Rochelle Turoff Mucha
Insight is a step toward sel
voking, funny, sad, and po
each of our own personalities. I highly recommend that you read this
masterpiece of human experience from someone who has truly lived
the gift of time weaving her lifetime moments into a meaningful pattern of relationship, special memories and personal history. This is a
must-read for each of us who are in relationships now, who WANT to
be in relationships and who are fulfilled just by being who we are.

Linda Wind CEO Possible Woman Enterprises, Chair, Possible
Woman Foundation International

To read Rochelle's book, **Men and Me**, is to appreciate her authenticity as she shares challenges she encountered and lessons learned
throughout her journey as a single woman. Anyone still searching for
"Mr. Right" can certainly benefit from her rich and varied experiences!

Bonnie Ross-Parker, Author, Walk In My Boots –
The Joy of Connecting

Men and Me is a wonderfully detailed account of the challenges we
face in relationships---I suspect that everyone will recognize themselves in these intriguing tales. Rochelle Turoff Mucha's uniquely
engaging writing style illuminates many examples of the joys and frus-
trations of dating. She shares her insights and lessons related to the
ways in which we all unconsciously sabotage our relationships. Enjoy
this book the next time you are looking for something to read that is
entertaining, easy-to-read and also meaningful!

Dr. Deanna Berg,President,
Innovation Strategies International

Men and Me is the first book I have read that describes the personal maturity of a woman through dating. I put dog-ears on so many
pages because the insights resonated so strongly for me. I personally
could identify with either the insight or the emotion. For me it was lessons that I didn't receive growing up, either from my own mom or
friends. It helped me to realize the journey I have been on and be
clearer about what I want.

Ashley Keith, fellow explorer

Men and Me

Entertainment *to* Insight

Rochelle Turoff Mucha

Llumina Press

ISBN: 1-932560-62-9
Printed in the United States of America by Llumina Press

Dedication

To the women in my life, my family, friends and fellow explorers in the search for entertainment and insight.

Acknowledgements

Friendship amongst women is special, and I applaud all of my friends, who throughout the years have encouraged me to write my story. Several of you took the time to review the early stages of my book. I appreciate my best friend and sister, Carol Schrift, lifetime friend Patti Brave and dear kindred spirits Elizabeth Wood, Ashley Keith and Pilar Nerenberg.

I would not be here if not for my mother, who brought me into this world and gave me unconditional love. Now approaching ninety, you are a model of grace and dignity.

The words that come to mind when I think of my editor, Arlene Robinson, are Energy, Enthusiasm and Encouragement. All this and talent too. Thank you! Thank you! Thank you!

This story is about the men in my life. Without them, this book would not have been possible. I smile on your contributions.

The primary "man" for most of my life is my son. Thank you for your love, humor, resiliency and wisdom. Not by your choice, you have played many roles in my journey, and I love you for being with me even when you didn't want to.

Finally, to "my pickle man," the one that wouldn't budge, my husband, best friend, lover and life partner. The simple word "love" is nowhere near enough to express what I feel for you, and why. It took an entire book.

Men and Me

Entertainment *to* Insight

Table of Contents

Live with intention, walk to the edge, play with abandon, choose with no regret, appreciate your friends, practice vitality, do what you love, live as if this is all there is.

Mary Anne Hershey

I must learn to love the fool in me — the one who feels too much, talks too much, takes too many chances, wins sometimes and loses often, lacks self control, loves and hates, hurts and gets hurt, promises and breaks promises, laughs and cries. He alone protects me against that utterly self-controlled masterful tyrant whom I also harbor and who would rob me of human aliveness, humility and dignity but for my fool.

Theodore Isaac Rubin

Introduction

Men and **Me:** Entertainment *to* Insight

Dating is a form of entertainment. Like a movie. Some good. Some bad. Some wonderful, romantic, seductive. Some funny, light, an excellent escape. Some provocative. Some movies you can see over and over and over again. Some… once is enough!

Men are a form of entertainment. Some people gasp when I say this. Others laugh. Some think it is insulting. I don't. I think it is honest, and I have plenty of experience to back up my point of view.

Don't misunderstand or misinterpret my observation. I like men a lot! That's why I have lots of experience *dating*. However, to sustain and survive in my quest for Mr. Right, I was compelled to find *humor* amid my frustration.

I turned fifty-three this year. At nineteen, I married my first husband. I was twenty-four when we separated with a four-year-old son, and legally divorced two years later. I was fifty-one when I married again: nearly twenty-seven years of being single after my first marriage.

You may be wondering, "What compels a woman to remarry after being on her own for twenty-seven years?"

Twenty-seven years provides a lot of experience. It is a lifetime. Yet this is *not* a story with an explicit message. I think it isn't really a story at all. It is my memories… my amazing memories of loves, near loves and no loves. It is what happened in between my first and second marriage. It describes the *real* world of a most typical single woman struggling to find her way. It is a tale of my personal, social and sexual maturity. It is triumphant, yet bittersweet.

Some of you may remember *Waiting to Exhale,* a wonderful

novel by Terry McMillan. I read this book in 1992, and even though I frequently cannot remember what I did yesterday, I clearly remember one memorable page (at least for me) in that book. It was page eleven, when the main character, Savannah, is preparing for a blind date. Savannah is fretting, like most of us do on these occasions. She explains to her readers how she used to pray to G-d to send her a *"decent* man." And that "he did."

After many *decent* men, she learned that she needed to be more exact: that she'd left out some important attributes, such as *"compassion, pride versus cockiness* and *confidence versus arrogance."* Savannah goes on to tell her readers that now her prayers are more detailed. She asks for a man that will *"talk about what he feels; have a genuine sense of purpose in life; a sense of humor* and *is already what he wants to be, rather than what he is aspiring to be."*

Savannah doesn't stop there. She adds, "Let him be *honest, responsible, drug-free, a little spontaneous, full of zest, good-looking enough* and of course *a passionate lover.*

"Her prayers now take forever, but she is not taking any chances."

I learned as well. Although I was not praying to G-d for a man (I had bigger, more urgent issues for G-d such as courage, direction, strength and basic shelter), I did have a list of needs, wants and desires that grew with my age and experiences. I started with a short list: *smart, humorous, passionate.* I added *likes their job* when I realized I couldn't tolerate a man complaining every day about his work. And a decade later I added, *enjoys a healthy lifestyle,* as it became apparent many men didn't like watching me eat tofu, yet alone dare to share a tofu meal.

I am sure most of you recall the evolution of your own lists; it's what most of us do during the "in-between time" of relationships. We think a lot, trying to understand what went wrong. Our lists become one way we rationalize why any given relationship didn't work, a way to say, "We didn't fail. The man just didn't match our requirements."

Writing this book has been a wonderful experience for me in revisiting my past with both pride and remorse. I have always been a *thinker*, a person who *reflects*. One of the men friends I met along the way gave me a gift after we spent some time talking together. It was a book: *The Prophet*, by Kahlil Gibran. He enclosed a letter to me that remains inside the book. A part of his letter reads:

> . . . *I have been thinking about your concepts and feelings regarding the quality of life. Most people don't consider or even develop the quality of their lives. They are satisfied with the here and now. The routines and ruts of life.*

He had a point. I suppose I've always been searching, thinking aloud on how to make my life better, how to understand myself more. Along the way I've accumulated much evidence that my audible struggle has touched others in a good and profound way. I predict and hope it will touch you.

My journey as a single woman has had many stops. Some tales are funny. Some sad. Some indiscreet. Some I am not terribly proud of. I loved. I was loved. I played. I hurt. I learned. I grew. I trust you will find a bit of yourself in my tales. Parts may make you smile. Or frown. Feel good about yourself. Or want desperately to forget. Thank you for joining me on my trip down memory lane.

In the Beginning . . .

There are no maps, only compasses.

Anonymous

T he setting is New York. I am twenty-four, newly separated, making my first entry as a single woman. I am *fresh, romantic, optimistic* and *naïve*. I am wide-eyed and tremendously ignorant. I believe in love, passion, and romance—everything I perceived I didn't have during my brief marriage. Divorce, reduced income and a "meat boycott" combined to accidentally cause me to lose ten pounds without dieting. I am reveling in a welcome and novel experience of feeling *thin*. I was young, a single mother, and on my own for the first time in my life.

This would have been daring enough, but it was also the seventies, a wild and crazy time still reeling from the impact of the Vietnam War and the feminist movement.

Most girls I knew grew up in high school and college. *Sexually* grew up, that is. I missed that. I was a virgin when I first married, and even in 1968, this was unique. Remaining a virgin wasn't necessarily my choice. I had plenty of opportunity with my high-school boyfriend of three years. But he wouldn't *do it* with a girl he respected. And the one and only boyfriend I had in my freshmen year of college before I met my husband wouldn't either. Even a ski weekend in Vermont didn't change his mind. Everyone else skied; being a purely warm-weather person, I focused on hot chocolate, not the slopes. He would *literally* sleep with me, but not *go all the way*.

So I entered and departed my marriage with very little sexual experience. Being perceived as innocent proved to be both a blessing and a handicap. My first lover after my separation was older and very Italian. He told me that if it weren't for the fact I had a son, he would've thought I was still a virgin. That statement captures the sexual life of my first marriage.

It begins now. The men of my first chapter. My teachers. My guides. My entertainment, if you will, for the next twenty-seven years....

LIMO GUY

Older and Italian. I was completely in awe, totally engaged. I felt my high-school loafers shed as I transformed into a mature woman.

The first time we made love, I did what I always did when I was married: I undressed in the bathroom, came out covered, snuck into the bed hoping not to have my nakedness exposed.

Was I experienced or what? I can only guess what he must have been thinking. Thank goodness for his patience. Perhaps I was one of his many students. When my Limo Guy made love to me (which also was my *oral sex* inauguration), I nearly fainted. *Can this feeling be real?* I remember thinking.

I couldn't get enough of this perceived ecstasy, felt powerless to the chills that ran inside the length of my body: an internal shiver that is warm rather than cold. I never wanted this feeling of freedom to end, and when it did, I wanted it again and again. This feeling I desired so much became more important than the face of the provider.

After several weeks, he told me that one day, my next husband would send him a thank-you note in appreciation for the sensual and capable woman I had become. That he had taught me everything I would ever need to know.

Unfortunately, it took so long to identify my next husband that I no longer knew where to send the note. Still, my current husband expresses his gratitude and if given the chance, would not only thank him but also ask him for some additional tips.

Limo Guy taught me more than just the mechanics of sex. Once, we went out to dinner to celebrate the holiday season. I was a girl from Brooklyn, grew up in a working-class home. Lobster was a rare treat, and it was on the menu. Timidly—a departure from my normal assertive self—I asked permission to order it.

He laughed, then instructed me: "Any time a man invites you

out for dinner, you feel free to order anything on the menu. If he does not anticipate that, then he should not be taking you to that restaurant."

I never forgot his lesson.

Limo Guy earns his name because he ran the limousine service that picked my son up at preschool and brought him to the community center where I worked. Just goes to prove early-on, you never know where you might meet someone. He claims many firsts—one of which is being my first married man, a pattern I hardly knew I was starting at the time. Although we were not lovers then, I did know him before I separated from my husband. In retrospect, I'll never know just how much his attention and flirtation contributed to the end of my first marriage.

What I *do* know is that he sparked flames in me I had never felt before. Heat I could never imagine. When he looked at me, for the first time in my twenty-four years I felt beautiful, sexy and desirable. I had always viewed myself as plain, smart, perhaps cute, but never pretty. Compared to my pencil-thin school-days friends, I always felt chubby. In a mirror's reflection I frequently saw myself as huge.

I will never forget a remark made about me by a fellow high-school boy at a senior party. My back was to him, and he turned to a friend and commented on the "amazing breadth" of my butt. It still hurts. Smarts as if it happened yesterday. Like many of you, my struggles with dieting and self-image challenges seem to be a lifetime endeavor. Even though I was always popular and not lacking for girl or boy friends, I never considered going after the best-looking guys: the *golden rings*. I was confident I would make a fool of myself.

Limo Guy achieved the first big chisel-mark on that mindset. He began the evolution of me, from a girl to a woman.

HANDSOME NEIGHBOR

SO HANDSOME! A definite *golden ring!* Exactly the kind of man I would admire from a distance, envy the girl on his arm and then remind myself why I could never be that girl. Too fat! Too plain! Too unfashionable! Too! Too! Too! I wasn't the type of woman who gets the attention of HANDSOME. Cognitively, I knew I was no longer the high-school chubbette, but emotionally I wasn't attached to my now-size-eight figure either.

Proximity fostered this meeting. After my son was born, my husband and I moved to a larger apartment on the other end of Ocean Parkway, not far from the Atlantic Ocean. It was a definite step up, and in the right direction. We added a bedroom, bathroom and terrace to our space. It felt luxurious to me, and I remained there after our divorce.

I knew Handsome Neighbor before and after my marriage; he and his family lived in the same apartment building. When he first came on to me, I could hardly believe it. I turned around, looking to see who was behind me. Certainly he wasn't flirting with me! Yet his flattery was enticing and delighted me, especially since his wife had frequently shunned my offer of friendship.

For some time, I had admired this man with dark hair and a deep complexion bearing a thin but sturdy frame, had stood next to him often, but had always felt invisible beside him. There was no saying *no*, despite how many legitimate and important reasons there were to say *no*. The retailer was married, and this self-defeating pattern surfaced again.

Our fling was clandestine and extremely short-lived. As handsome as he was, Handsome Neighbor was shallow: not a street or academic smart in him. Through conversation and lovemaking, he demonstrated how self-serving and arrogant he was. I needed time, not fleeting, terse attention.

I look back now, trying to understand my own behavior and choices. I can only rationalize that I needed to have someone like him in my life, even if it *was* briefly. Fantasizing about what it would be like to win a HANDSOME man far exceeded the experience of attaining him. A lesson well learned.

SHOE SALESMAN

From handsome to practical.

When my son was little, my only means of transportation during the day was my bike equipped with a seat on the back of it. For those of you not familiar with Brooklyn, it is pretty big. I used to peddle my way, perhaps twenty miles or so, to the shoe store where I bought my son's shoes. It was the same store where my mother had taken me. On that fateful August day the owner's son, who was visiting from Maryland, was manning the store.

At this time in my life, Maryland was an unfamiliar place. Little did I know or could foresee that just two years later I would be living in the same zip code as his daughter, literally bumping into him on airplanes.

Back to the present. One bright, sunny August day, I arrived at the shoe store. I was all decked out. Shorts. Halter-top. Pigtails. Sweat dripping down my forehead from pedaling the distance. I looked about twelve, not twenty-four. He was older, sophisticated, wore *regular, grown-up* shoes, not penny loafers. When he asked me out during the charge card process, I was stunned. Feeling stunned was my normal reaction to flirtation at this stage of my life and singleness; I didn't see myself as attractive. From that day, I became his work in progress, his Pygmalion.

Unlike Limo Guy, Shoe Salesman didn't teach me anything about sex. Well, I shouldn't say that. He taught me the value of *faking* it. This became easy to do. I simply fantasized myself back with Limo Guy, and moved and mouthed accordingly.

But Shoe Salesman more than made up for this with wonderful lessons on how to be treated like a lady. He personified chivalry, knew the art of spoiling a woman. He introduced me to wine. He knew how to speak to women (girls, sisters, mothers, grandmothers) and simply lured them. Though not handsome, Shoe Salesman's funny features became interesting signs of character because of his charm.

Our first date was another teaching moment for me. We arrived at our destination, and as usual I let myself out of the car. Wrong move! He lectured me on how I had to wait until he came around and opened the car door.

This was a novel idea for me, but seemed easy enough to do. However, it raised my expectations of other men. I cannot begin to tell you how many times I waited in a car while my date went on ahead, hardly noticing I was absent. Consequently, I adopted a new habit. Whenever I went out on a date, upon arriving at our destination, I would ask, "Are you the kind of man who opens car doors, or should I get out on my own?"

Most times, I got chuckles. Then, found my way out.

Shoe Salesman wasn't married, but wasn't really available. He had an "on and off" steady. It would not be the last time that I was the *off*-girl. As I look back on my shoe salesman I think of a good friend, little thrills, great dinners.

The universe brought people into my life that I needed. This wasn't clear to me until decades later, when I came to realize that I was blessed with the teachers and assistants I needed, at the time I needed them.

SUV GENT

My first year as a single woman seemed dominated by older men, each taking me under their wing. SUV Gent was an exception. We met through a common friend. Although there were no fireworks, I urgently wanted to be with someone who was truly single and unencumbered, so I feigned enthusiasm.

Wherever we went out, he would point out Jeeps as we drove. Maybe that was the only kind of SUV at the time. In any case, I would get an animated description of them along with his longing for one. I am sure by now he has accomplished that task.

SUV Gent was the only legitimate *available* male I dated during year one. No girlfriends. No wives. No pets. Yet my feigned enthusiasm couldn't be sustained. Even now, as I write, I'm challenged to recall something memorable about him. I remember how proud he was of his morning breakfast routine. Two slices of dry rye toast and fruit. I think he might have been my first *healthy lifestyle* friend, but all this happened before *healthy lifestyle* made my list.

We were never serious. Never sexual. SUV Gent was mundane; I wasn't at all ready for "mundane." There were no crazy-and-wild college memories for me. I was married and pregnant during college, a mother before I graduated. I never even attended my own graduation ceremonies. I can see now that I needed to create memories. I didn't want ordinary, comfortable. I wanted *adventure. Entertainment.*

How wise I am now. Hindsight is always twenty-twenty. (Words do become clichés for a reason.)

California Dreamers

*The great thing in this world is not so much where we are,
but in what direction we are moving.*

Oliver Wendall Holmes

LA CELEBRITY

Year two was spectacular. It was during this time that some of my girlhood fairy tales became reality, even if only for a brief time.

When I was a little girl, California was a distant, magical land. I had grown up on the Mouseketeers. My family was middle-class. We lived in an apartment building in Brooklyn. All four of us shared one bathroom. I didn't go away to summer camp. We didn't have a car. (It is a myth that New Yorkers don't need cars. This is only true if you are financially comfortable and/or live in Manhattan, not Brooklyn. Most of my friend's families had cars, and a welcomed gift for me was to be invited to go along on a car trip to the zoo, or even the library. Actually, just anywhere.)

I had my first car after I was married, and shared that with my husband who used it for work. My main transportation was the bicycle with the toddler seat on the back. For the first twenty years after my separation I was the not-so-proud owner of a long list of used cars.

Returning to my California story. I was teaching so I could have the same hours as my son, who was now in school. I saved my pennies and planned a trip to California during winter break. This was my dream trip. All my life, I had wanted to go to California. My alter ego had always been on stage, yet the Hollywood life seemed unattainable from where I sat in Brooklyn. I wasn't raised to create and follow dreams. Now, I was on my way.

My son, who was six going on thirty and a very friendly sort, started up a conversation with this somewhat disheveled-looking guy at the then-Idlewild Airport, now known as JFK. Although described by most as "friendly" and perhaps even "intense," "assertive" and "loquacious," I have a serious intro-

verted side. This side usually takes over wher
on this day at the airport I was in my own
wasn't interested in small talk with a fleeti
immersed in living out my dream.

As luck would have it—and it *was* luck—
wound up sitting next to us on the plane. I soon discovered wนat
a pleasant, smart and interesting man he was. Some five hours
later as we prepared to land, he invited my son and me to dinner
that evening.

This was the seventies, before the age of paranoia. Life was
simpler then. I wasn't worried about him being a serial killer or
terrorist, so I accepted.

I explained that my wardrobe was rather limited. I had jeans
and more jeans. He said fine, and we all agreed to meet at seven
in the lobby of my hotel.

Right on time, we met and walked out to his car, and this is
where my California fantasy began to take on life. He drove a
Rolls Royce.

You see, the somewhat disheveled man on the plane was
worn out after returning home from India and other faraway
places. He was an author of travel books. He was also an attorney. He had a radio show with his girlfriend, and they had
published a book together that addressed jealousy and posses-
siveness in relationships (literally the book turned upside-down
halfway, each half speaking from the opposite gender's view).

Our first stop included a stroll through a bookstore, where I
skimmed through LA Celebrity's other short books. Most were
self-help texts written to advise consumers on the current marijuana laws, and to empower renters to outsmart their
landlords… or, if you were a landlord, how to outsmart your
tenant. I could tell he had a knack for paradox.

I didn't want to wake up from this dream. The bad news—
LA Celebrity had a significant other. The good news—he wasn't
married. It was my vacation, and I was in Beverly Hills. I gave
myself some slack for misbehavior. This local celebrity played
tour guide and host for my son and me a few more times during

sit, during the off-time with my other California dream
r that appeared during my stay. It was this other lover who
ould follow me from LA to San Diego.

FANTASY IN SAN DIEGO

My son's kindergarten teacher was a kindred spirit: young, divorced, a single parent of a boy my son's age. She was a "with it" person: someone I would have never been friends with in high school or college. Someone who would have never wanted me as a friend. I was too square. Yet at this time of my life, she was exactly what I needed and wanted. (The universe brings what or whom we need, male or female, if we are able to see and welcome it.)

Before I left for California, she gave me the telephone number of a male friend of hers. He had recently separated from his wife and children and moved back to his parent's home outside Southern LA. He was "very fresh and wounded." She encouraged me to call, and I did. On so many levels, I'm glad I did.

Fantasy in San Diego was an absolute gorgeous hunk, but unlike Handsome Neighbor, had substance and heart. Although there was no lasting attraction on his part for me, he was hungry for his children and completely drawn to my son. That was easy to do, since my son was, and is, the kind of person who draws people to him. I met both of my California dream-loves because of my son, who remains completely charismatic when he wants to be.

Fantasy in San Diego doted on us. He took us on a tour of *his* California, and to his home. We had family meals, and experienced the natives who did not "hang" in Beverly Hills. Five days later, my son and I drove down to San Diego, where we planned to stay until after New Year's Day. He drove down to spend New Year's Eve with us.

This was a first for me. Two men within a two-week time frame. But I felt no guilt, just euphoria. I didn't feel belittled; I felt empowered. I felt beautiful.

We left the next day, headed back home to New York. Leaving California was the only trip I have ever cried coming home from. *If only my life could be like this vacation!* I thought. *If only I could find the adventure and passion in New York that I found in California.*

I got on a plane and never heard from either one of those guys again. I'm sure they remain far more unforgettable to me than I was to them.

Back Home, Back to Reality

The longest journey is the journey inward.

Dag Hammarskjold

DISTRICT ATTORNEY

As I travel down this dating journey, I'm sure the personal insecurity I grappled with is evident. You might have picked up by now that although popular, I never thought of myself as "hot." I didn't go after the handsome or celebrated men. And although academically accomplished in school, I didn't feel professional, sophisticated. Men who were especially educated or held important positions easily intimidated me.

Perhaps these perceived inadequacies stemmed from the fact that my father didn't graduate high school, and my mother, though smart, headed to work after graduating high school to help support her family during the Depression. High goals weren't discussed or encouraged in our house, and I was the first person in my family to graduate college, earn two post-college degrees, move out of New York, own a home, own a car and run my own business.

After getting to know me and my "story," people have frequently asked me, "Why (and how) did you get where you are?"

Some proclaim I have courage. I don't think so. I think I was and am irreverent, and I know I'm stubborn, frequently even defiant. I was favored with wonderful friends who played a large role in inspiring me. I always knew what I *didn't* like, and was quick to get up and leave. The problem is, I really didn't know what I *liked*.

So what does this have to do with District Attorney?

I'm back from California, and in the world of New York dating. The prospect of a blind date with a New York district attorney who lived on the Upper West Side was daunting. My recall of my anticipation far exceeds my recall of him.

I drove up to meet him at his townhouse on a Sunday. Then we drove to visit some close friends of his in nearby Connecticut. They had a small place that sat on the water. A boat. A hammock. When I went to find the bathroom, I exposed my ignorance instead. I had never seen a bathroom with two rooms before. I would open the door and see a sink, and was sure I was missing something. It was more than slightly embarrassing to have to be escorted through the next door where the toilet was.

The day was filled with idle chatter. I frequently felt excluded from what appeared to be fraternal and familiar conversation. These accomplished people left me bored and longing for the day to end.

This was the beginning of my second year as a single woman. I was getting weary of dating and feeling so insignificant. I was beginning to want more — to feel disenchanted with my new-found freedoms.

The last thing I remember about District Attorney was the lonely drive home that Sunday night. It was still light out. I cried the whole time.

I decided to escape the seventies mentality. Get serious! Foolishly, I thought I was closer to knowing what I wanted and needed.

Wishful thinking. I did not.

ENCYCLOPEDIA MAN

Following my son's footsteps, I had moved on from teaching at the preschool at the community center to teaching first grade. Daycare was neither available nor affordable, and my son was now in first grade, so I paralleled his schedule so I could deliver him in the morning and pick him up in the afternoon.

Many single people meet others where they work. One fine day, Encyclopedia Man came to visit my classroom to present some information on, of course, the encyclopedia. (Remember, this was pre-Internet. Paper was in.)

My class learned about the wonders of research, and I got a date, and more. The "more" was a great trip to Mexico. I was at my thinnest, and still prize one of the only pictures I've ever had taken of me in a bikini that I even admire. Cognitively, I know it was me. But since in my head I will forever be a "chubbette," I look at the woman in the picture as a stranger: someone else, not me.

Encyclopedia Man was single, and crazy for me. He volunteered to perform a magic show at my son's birthday party, and was a huge hit with the audience. He wanted to marry me. My first genuine prospect of remarriage. A positive. But this guy was fond of pot, and I don't mean the kind you cook in. A big disconnect for me. Anyway, how could you marry someone who cuts his toenails and leaves the clippings on the carpet?

I had amassed a list of all the reasons why I should not, could not marry this man, all of which contributed to my sense of flight. It was time to end this romance—and as it would turn out, it was also time to leave New York. And I did.

Baltimore Memories

Experience is the name everyone gives to their mistakes.

Oscar Wilde

When people ask me how I got to Maryland, my wiseass response is to say "By car." Most people relocate for a job, or marriage. Something compelling. I had none of these traditional reasons. Yet it all seemed so logical at the time. My former husband remarried. His new wife asked him to choose between his son and her. He chose her. That left me in New York, twenty-six years old, raising a little boy alone. It was costly, and not pretty. I was eager to simplify and beautify my life. California here I come, searching to recapture my fantasy and create a new life.

We all know what happens to best-laid plans. They change. I never made it to California. Here's why: Before finalizing my plans, I visited my dearest friends in Maryland, a couple I met on the first of two vacations with my former husband. Just as they appeared to be at Club Med (our first meeting), my friends were and remain the most *perfect* couple. They embody all those enviable, yet hard-to-attain attributes of a successful marriage: love, romance, support, communication, fun and more.

Among the many things my Maryland friends enjoyed together was a dynamic sex life. It was during a visit I made to them while married that I discovered *Penthouse* magazine: an experience that proved to be a catalyst for my major life change. Till then, *Penthouse* was a magazine I had seen on the stands but never looked inside. Although curious, I wasn't going to be caught glancing at *Penthouse* while browsing the newsstand. Now, looking at the pictures in *Penthouse* (and that's what I was doing, not reading the articles), I was overwhelmed and intrigued.

Ah, ha! I thought. My reaction to the explicit photos in *Penthouse* accounted for why after my divorce Limo Guy told me he would've thought me a virgin had he not known my son.

My quest to learn more compelled me to speak with my friends about what I saw, and doing so validated my intuition about the void in my own marriage and sexual life. Knowing them, and knowing what I knew now from *Penthouse*, I yearned for a marriage that would be more than just comfortable and provide companionship.

I've always said that this wonderful couple was the reason I got a divorce, and the reason I didn't remarry for a long time — their *perfect* marriage was what I wanted. But their bar proved exceedingly high to reach.

During this current visit, my friends tried to influence my thinking. "California is so far from family and friends!" they would tell me. I wasn't convinced, but agreed to look at apartments near them, and got hooked on a brand-new garden apartment with a yellow kitchen, my then-favorite color. The apartment was in a lovely suburb outside of Baltimore, where you could actually see the grass when you looked outside your window. The rent was half what I was paying in New York. The absolute best was that the school bus would pick my son up in the morning and bring him home in the afternoon. My crack-of-dawn transportation responsibilities back home — rising early to get my son to school, schlepping cross-town to get me to work and back again every day, rain, sleet or snow — would end.

The decision seemed self-evident, so I allowed myself to see it and be swayed.

To date, at age twenty-six, it seemed like I had been a prisoner of the fifth floor. All three of my apartments so far — the apartment I was born and raised in and the two I lived in while married — were on the same avenue in Brooklyn, and all three were on the fifth floor. This new place didn't feel like an apartment, but like a home, and I was ready to escape. Impulsive and naïve, I made a quick decision and signed on the dotted line.

I returned to New York, packed up our stuff (not much), got in my car and drove to Maryland. This was a major family event, given that I was the first person in our family to leave New York.

The sad send-off was planned at one of Brooklyn's many fabulous diners, The Four Corners. My mother claims to this day that I left without turning back, never taking that last look or giving that last wave. She was right. I found that I was adept at leaving.

It's critical to mention here that, before ever looking for a home outside of New York, I had consulted with my son's dad about the potential move. Given his lack of interest and involvement, it was fine with him. That was, until I moved. Then I suddenly became guilty of breaking our divorce agreement and preventing his visitation. He stopped sending me the small amount of child support and alimony legally due to me. I arrived in Maryland with my son and no job or income. But there was no turning back, only looking forward.

Others hear my story and see me as bold and fearless. I maintain that I was ignorant, and in this case ignorance was not always bliss. I had no job. I had no money. I rest my case. I wasn't brave; I was immature and foolish. To this day, I marvel how it all worked out okay. Perhaps because my prayers for courage, strength, direction and basic shelter were answered.

I spent six years in Baltimore, a great small town. As the city was growing, so was I. I arrived at twenty-six and left at thirty-two. So much happened. At the beginning, I often felt like a lost soul, a stranger. But at the end it was *home*.

It was Baltimore where I had my first true love and loss. (More on that later.)

It was Baltimore where I moved from the schoolroom to the corporate room.

It was Baltimore where my son first flourished, then declined, leading to one of the most painful moments and separations of my life.

Although this recollection of my journey is not about my trials and tribulations as a single mother, they are always there in the background. For any readers who have been down that path, you will appreciate my expression that my son and I grew up together. And this was not to his benefit! He was my son, my best friend, companion and, all too often, husband substitute, in that he frequently had to deal with my financial and emotional distress. Too many roles for a little boy.

But don't misread me. I was a good, better-than-good parent, guilty of only loving and needing my son too much.

Let's return to the juicier stuff. My life as a single mom of a wonderful but frequently challenging little boy wasn't easy. The men who came into my life offered me an escape from a difficult daily reality. I took it. Dating became my *entertainment*, because I wasn't ready for anything else.

QUEEN OF BLIND DATES

The only people I knew in Maryland were happily married couples. I soon became the new girl in town, referred to every available man known to their circle of friends. My record number of blind dates is an unrecognized achievement in the *Guinness Book of World Records.*

Like Savannah in *Waiting to Exhale*, blind dates were always nerve-wrecking. Despite my intellectual self-talk, I frequently found myself stalking this or that stranger, standing by the window in the dark, waiting for a glimpse so I could prepare myself to smile no matter what. I progressed to master these covert skills.

I didn't have high expectations of blind dates. Didn't anticipate getting wowed. They were a diversion. Someone to fill the time with until I met a *steady*. Being new to the city, they introduced me to restaurants and offered anecdotal stories about the community.

Not by design, I began to observe a pattern. Most men were extremely chivalrous and cordial on date *one*. They exemplified dating etiquette, and spoke like they were graduates of successful texts like *Men are from Mars and Women are from Venus*. This continued on date *two*. Somehow, on date *three*, things changed. At the end of date *three*, most men wanted more: more of me than I wanted to give. It felt like they expected me to *pay* for my dinner.

I had a lot of three-date blind dates. This became my private joke.

Most of these blind dates weren't significant. Here's a sample of one-timers:

👽 **Too Short to See**

I opened the door and looked down. I am five foot three. Being vulnerable to vanity has always been personally challenging. It makes me feel guilty, small, and shallow. After all, shouldn't I be bigger than worrying about how tall someone is? Why is it so important that I look up to my dates? Have I been listening to *Funny Girl* lyrics too many times?: "I am woman, and you are man; I am smaller so you can be taller than...."

I'm not proud to acknowledge that I strongly preferred taller and well-built to shorter, chunkier men. I think this preference was born out of my preoccupation with weight and size. In my mind, I could feel smaller with these men, a feeling I evidently needed a lot. Down the road there would be rare exceptions to this obsession, but not for *this* short man.

⑨ First Impressions?

I opened the door and my babysitter ran, laughing hysterically, to the other room. I had to calm her down before I felt safe to leave. Then I had to figure out where I could go with this person where I wouldn't see anyone I knew. Vanity strikes again! I hoped to have the depth and wisdom to discover his "great personality," but was fixated on his dumbo ears. This was no Halloween outfit. I worked harder, digging deep inside me to see beyond his appearance. I labored in vain.

🌡 Hot in the City!

Maryland gets rather humid in summer. This was a July date-night. All was well until we reached his car, a seasoned, *not* air-conditioned VW Beetle. My date opened the door but my body froze, planted to the cement ground envisioning a meltdown if I proceeded. I tactfully suggested we go in my car, which had air conditioning. He got angry. I inferred he thought I had unreasonable demands. If wanting to drive in an air-conditioned car in July is unreasonable, I confess: guilty as charged. We never left the parking lot . . . at least, not together.

✄ Handymen

Clichés surface with truth again. Consider, "It's so nice to have a man around the house." Occasionally I would get lucky and have what I call "handy dates" just when I needed them. There was the carpenter. A mover. An electrician. All of these skills were greatly welcomed. I would see them for dinner and in return, implore them to help me with household tasks that were outside my comfort zone. Install a fixture, connect the stereo system, put together furniture, unclog a drain, put in a new showerhead. That was the extent of the bartering, and usually worked okay.

Although most of these tasks were blue-collar, I sometimes found myself in need of an attorney. Shortly after moving to Maryland, I learned about Maryland's commendable and diligent approach to enforcing speeding limits the hard way. I support traffic enforcement. I don't speed. Back in Brooklyn, it wasn't possible to go faster than 25 miles per hour on a typical city street. Without constant bumper-to-bumper traffic, I just had more space to move. Nevertheless, I did take exception to being ticketed twice in my new neighborhood for going 35 miles per hour in a 25-mile-per-hour zone.

Given I had zero experience with speeding tickets, I was unaware that I was getting *points* for my recklessness, and less aware that those points would double or more my car insurance premiums, or (worst case) my license would be taken away.

Conveniently, I had just met an attorney.

He stands out in my mind for several reasons. I remember his big, bushy eyebrows, which made it distracting to talk with him. I always found myself wondering, *Does he see a shadow from the bulge of his eyebrow hair sticking out?*

When he gallantly offered to assist me with my

speeding-ticket dilemma by representing me in court, I was grateful—but not so grateful that I continued to date him after the court hearing.

I didn't think much of it at the time. Years later, after I had left Maryland and moved to Pennsylvania, I ran into him during a visit back to Maryland. I was having dinner with a friend when I noticed this man staring at me. He rose from his table and approached me, reintroduced himself, and then proceeded to tell me that his current rebound marriage was caused by my rejection of him.

That was a shocker. I was clueless. And I didn't feel responsible. He was an obscure memory for me, but I had obviously been more vivid a memory for him.

More valuable hindsight: You never know the impact you can have on someone's life.

But not all my blind dates were disappointments....

OLDER MAN

Toward the end of my first year, the caliber of my blind dates started to improve. It was around my birthday, and I was leaving for my critical third date with a fetching older man. He drove a Mercedes 450, a cool car to me. I was taken by his age and status. At the time, those assets made him powerful in my eyes.

I was nervous about this third date. I struggled with what to do, or not do. I predicted that sexual overtures were on his agenda. I entered the car, extended my hand for a proper handshake, and in an effort to keep my personal commitment to have sex with only steady beaus, I told Older Man the following:

"Thank you for the lovely dates, but experience tells me that tonight is the night. You will want more. I won't give it. And you will be history. I just wanted to let you know that I really enjoyed our time together."

He laughed.

I saw Older Man another three times, allowed sexual intimacy, and received a birthday gift too: a lovely gold pin I still have. He was *the exception to the three-date rule*, but unfortunately, not a keeper. The stuff it takes to sustain chemistry wasn't there on his part, and he soon ended our fleeting relationship.

A few years later, I saw Older Man at a function, married to a much younger woman. Maybe you've experienced a similar situation. When those things happen, I ruminate. *What is it I didn't have? What is it I didn't do? Why her, not me?* And I ask these questions whether I really liked the guy or not.

ROSE MAN

One of my most dramatic and compelling memories was created in Baltimore. The ultimate blind-date swap. A likeable guy took me to see a concert. Not one with music but a comedian: George Carlin. We double-dated. The other guy had a beard. Seemed well-off and pompous. The first attitude was okay, the second one wasn't, but both were beguiling to me at my level of maturity. Three months later my phone rang, and it was him.

That call changed my life. This relationship was about my futile attempts to fill unmet, barren, Freudian needs. It was the catalyst for a time of great love, and great grief. It brought bouquets of roses, and the stench of deceit.

I grew up in a matriarchal home where my father resided somewhere between the floor and the carpet matting. Physically he existed, but as a person he disappeared from my life after age eight. I thought of him as invisible and weak. I grew to deplore weakness. Like my mother, I was a strong female, and determined to avoid the dynamics of my parents' marriage.

I was convinced that I needed a stronger male in my life. And as before, I would prove myself wrong.

A strong female thinks she needs a stronger male. Weak men are unacceptable, too easily controlled, reinforcing both what a strong female loves and loathes about herself. Decades later, I would learn to embrace what I perceived as a man's weaknesses as complements to my strengths. His easiness would calm my intenseness. His laid-back attitude would create acceptable silence instead of frenzy. His lack of ambition would free up his energy to bolster mine. His blanket generosity would soften my rigid views.

The struggle for a strong female to find her mate can only end when she resolves her own dilemma. It is the woman who owns the problem, not the man. Even so, this future life lesson wasn't available to benefit me now.

The bearded guy was my Rose Man. The attraction wasn't about looks; it was all about the bewitching power of pure romance.

Our first date began with the gift of a rose. That wasn't especially unusual, since many men, true romantics and pretenders alike, do that. But then I had one at my door every day. That was unusual *and* alluring. On our second date, Rose Man insisted that I see where he was born. On our third date, he chivalrously carried me over a puddle. Instead of embarrassment, I felt the envy of others.

He took me to Carmel, California our second month together because I *just had* to see his favorite spot. He was strong. He was smart. He was rich. He was *in love with me*, or so I thought. I had arrived.

Well, not quite.

For a smart girl, I should be mortified to tell you this: The first time we made love, he asked me, "What makes you mad?" Then he proclaimed, "I never want to make you mad."

"Hair on the soap," I replied.

This childish and ludicrous answer preceded my reading of *Waiting to Exhale*. I should have said, "Infidelity! *That* makes me mad."

It took me one year to have my naiveté exposed. To discover that his business trips weren't all that he claimed. To the contrary, Rose Man was having a parallel and equal relationship with another woman, whose face is indelible in my memory but whose name completely escapes me. Everyone knew but me.

I did what any woman would. I cried; screamed; begged; groveled; left; forgave.

I felt betrayed. I literally found myself wandering in the wee hours of the morning in a stupor of disbelief. My head ached with fear by what I should or could do, but I was more frightened by what I lacked the courage to do—leave immediately!

And so the volleyball game began. We were *on*. We *were* off. We were *on*. We were *off*. This went on for years. And the years were filled with pain, hurt, and shame.

During the *on* time, I had some great meals, frequented theater and traveled to a lot of great places. We went to Israel and visited the Wailing Wall, where as tradition dictated, I placed a crumpled piece of paper in a crevice with my only prayer. The single-word prayer was, *Courage.*

I received nice jewelry. I visited the White House, and experienced both awe and delight in strawberries so large I concluded they had been given steroids.

During the *off*-time I cried so much and so hard that my body shook. Melancholy lyrics of the popular music chart defined my life and emotions, but gave me little comfort.

Off-times were frequently cruelly orchestrated. One New Year's Eve, Rose Man showered me with gifts, flowers, and a romantic evening at the symphony. The next morning, he left for *her* again. He thought himself noble and generous for giving me this final celebration. I felt reduced to nothing.

His mother hated me. She thought I was out for his money. I wasn't. Rose Man was one of the only men my son ever spent any time with, and my son hated him. We were rarely a threesome. I vaguely remember sitting in a movie theater with them once. My imagination may have been playing tricks on me, but I can recall feeling like I was being tugged, literally, in two completely different directions. Perhaps I was.

My recollections feel degrading in many ways. I look back and puzzle over how I could stand silent each time he would march into my bedroom and shove my clothes to the side of the closet as he made room for his precious garb. Or took a towel I used for bathing to clean his shoes.

What was I thinking? What was I afraid of? Where was my own self-worth? My self-esteem? My boundaries?

There should be something philosophical or poetic to make sense of this, but I know of none. Nearly five years later I left him and Baltimore, my flight caused by matters of money, not the heart. A year after my departure, when Rose Man beseeched me to come back, it was too late. I said no. Thank goodness. I just moved on.

Before I transport you to my next stop, let me tell you how I entertained myself during the *off*-Rose Man time. After all, a girl needs entertainment.

INSURANCE MAN

There came a time when I left my teaching job and headed for the business world. This was a painful and necessary decision. I worked in the inner city. As a reading and language specialist, my classes were filled with the children that other teachers could not, or chose not to deal with. I thought of some of them as my pre-*60 Minutes* kids. I suspected that one day in the future, I would see them behind bars being interviewed by Mike Wallace.

These kids required a lot of emotional energy, and I had a demanding son at home to take care of as well. Add to this equation a public educational system that really didn't get it, and the daily danger. (I was greeted by German Shepherd watchdogs when I showed up for work at 7:00 a.m.) The only solution was that it was time to find another way to earn a living.

Being somewhat rebellious and frequently impetuous, I left in the middle of a December day with no clue as to where I would go. First stop was a job as bookkeeper for a mall design firm. They fired me in one month. Second stop was a receptionist for a mental health hospital. It was a two-person office, with the only other sounds being the voices of disturbed patients. Third stop was the Kidney Foundation. I was a network representative—a liaison between the kidney dialysis office and the medical providers. It was a challenging role... and it was there that my path crossed with Insurance Man.

Eyes meet across a crowded room . . . another cliché, but that's exactly what ours did. We weren't dancing, though; we were at the same meeting.

I sincerely don't recall making the first step. However, I concede to weakness and succumbing to the flirtation of an adorable man. This adorable man also turned out to be married. The troublesome pattern manifested itself once more.

Insurance Man was sensual and had my attention. He pursued, and I allowed myself to be caught. I wrote poems for him.

I believed his lies because I wanted to. My personal rules were abandoned as I craved stolen moments of sexual encounters captured wherever we could find opportunity.

He was the first man to wash my hair. Such an ordinary and daily routine took on welcomed new meaning and feeling. Watching Robert Redford replicate that experience with Meryl Streep in the movie *Out of Africa* causes old juices to flow.

I buried the truth that I was just a stop on Insurance Man's journey through multiple lives and relationships. And one day, it was his last stop as he moved on.

Years after my departure from Baltimore, I met him for lunch. The magnetic hunk had become fat, and his hair had thinned almost to invisibility.

Soapbox Moment:

I know married women (though I'm not one of them) will scream disapproval when I suggest that when a married partner has a relationship outside of their marriage, the cause can be found in the individual or the marriage. I believe that married men (or married women) are responsible for their own decisions, not their single lovers. Yes, it *is* poor judgment for any single person to respond to or pursue a married person, but it is not infidelity. Blaming the single partner may just be denial on behalf of the married person, who rightfully feels betrayed.

I will get off my soapbox now.

The demise of my memories of former lovers also became a recurring trend. I learned through these trips back in time that some memories are best held onto as-is. Going back, trying to rekindle or rediscover, sometimes only leads you to lose the freedom to escape back to the fanciful keepsakes you had.

MALPRACTICE OFFENDER

I spent my summers at the local library. When I was ten I read the book, *Leopold and Loeb, Life plus Ninety-Nine Years*. This was the true story of two teens and how they conspired to commit the perfect crime. I was captivated by the puzzle of criminal law. I wanted to be an *attorney*. I envisioned myself poised, articulate and powerful in court.

I could say that this notion never materialized because no one encouraged me. Maybe somewhat true, but that would be a cop-out. Whatever the reason, the truth is, I never thought of myself as a professional anything, and I seemed to lack the requisite ambition and self-confidence. In lieu of this goal, I became a lifetime viewer of *Law & Order* (every recent version included) and *Perry Mason*.

When my role at the Kidney Foundation ended, I answered an ad in the local paper for a legal assistant. The attorney who interviewed and then hired me told me he would send me to law school if I "worked out."

I was beside myself. Whimsically, I believed my childhood aspiration would come true. It felt like I had won the lottery.

Once again, my assumptions proved erroneous.

"Working out" meant "satisfying his every bizarre need."

Let me explain. I arrived on my first day all giddy with excitement, eager to talk with everyone. Immediately, I noticed that the women were not only silent, but seemed to be banished to peripheral offices. This was true for everyone except one tall blond, who was constantly by the lawyer's side.

The mystery soon unfolded. During my first meeting with him, Malpractice Offender attempted to slip a fifty-dollar bill down my blouse. I rejected him then, and every other attempt.

This was my first exposure to sexual harassment, an advance fueled by one, but nurtured by the silent collusion of others. Soon, I was banished too. I got my paycheck but little else.

Feeling disillusioned, I knew my days were numbered. I wasn't an attorney. I wasn't a secretary. I was useless. I was bored.

I lasted until November. That day, Malpractice Offender's right-hand yes-man visited each cubby and offered every employee a turkey: a token of Good Thanksgiving. I was tempted to throw it back in his face. Instead, I left. It had nothing to do with the fact that I was predominantly a vegetarian and did not eat poultry attached to its owner.

No law school for me, but another lesson learned.

SUPERMARKET ADVENTURES

Most single people have heard the advice of some dating gurus: If you want to meet someone single, hang out in the frozen section of your supermarket. (Singles equal frozen dinners.)

I actually tried it on several occasions. I would pick an upscale market. (If you are going to meet someone, might as well target someone who can afford gourmet.) But since I suffer from Raynaud's Syndrome (cold fingers and toes), lingering around the frozen section wasn't a comfortable idea, and I habitually went home with numb fingers rather than a date. Predictably, my Supermarket Adventures didn't result from any of my planned searches.

☒ Fastidious Man

My first Supermarket Man was someone I had previously seen at a party but hadn't spoken to at length. Irresistible. Also an exception to my "short bias." Assuming I wouldn't be of interest to him, I made no contact with him. The week after the party, we literally collided in a grocery aisle.

Familiarity was instant, and I was flattered that he had noticed me, too, and remembered our casual connection. After one date, Fastidious Man invited me to join him on a weekend business trip to Boston. Since I had never been to Boston, I said yes.

During the day I toured and walked, and he worked. In the evenings, we dined. It was during one of those lovely meals that he dropped the news that there was a "special lady" in his life. His timing sucked. Although not married, he was "emotionally attached."

We saw each other during our mutual *off*-times. Déjà vu. We also became friends. Amazing how complementary the world can be. Before leaving Maryland

I found myself in transition, and literally homeless. Fastidious Man offered me his place, since he was out of town for an extended time.

I remember his painstaking instructions on how to clean the dryer vent. He was a little obsessed with this. Each time he would call to say hello, he asked me whether I had cleaned it. *Very* fastidious! I stayed at his place two months, and abide by his lessons on cleaning the lint filter to this day.

✤ Checkout Guy

My second Supermarket Man swept me off my feet as I did my fruit-shopping, which I take very seriously. To this day, I load my fruit meticulously in the section of the cart created for toddlers to sit. My own precious cargo is fruit.

Our meeting was brief. I was at the checkout, decked out in my Peter Pan outfit (no makeup, baseball cap, sunglasses). He lived in New Orleans.

We corresponded, and I fell in *something* through our letter-writing. Checkout Guy convinced me to visit him for the most important date night in the whole year: New Year's Eve. Here is a good example of how fantasy and reality are not the same: The date was *so bad* that I left his apartment in the middle of the night and flew home.

As expected, the person I was most mad at was me. How foolish I felt! Feeling foolish was somewhat of a recurring theme with me. Although I know I made the best decisions I could at the time, it seemed that I often felt pretty stupid. I questioned then, and even now, how such a *smart* girl could be so *dumb* about men.

Biding Time in Pittsburgh

I always view problems as opportunities in work clothes.

Henry Kaiser

Would I ever grow up? Would I ever make good decisions when it came to men? Would I ever get married again? Have more children? Live a conventional life? Be part of a couple?

I was unraveling, and felt as if I had no control. I had no job. Again. I had no income. Again. My son was in trouble and seemed to need what I couldn't give him. My relationships had bombed. Disappointments seemed to fill my life.

I stopped and reflected about what I truly liked. Books. School. Education. These comprised my only safe haven. I could have been a perennial student.

I began to think about the publishing industry. My former brother-in-law was in publishing, so I called him. He told me about the role of a publishing representative. This role represented a specific publisher, and focused on sales, marketing and editorial work.

I was intrigued. Given my experience as a teacher (I held a master's degree in language and reading education) I was certain that my interests and credentials would lead me toward "EL-HI" (elementary through high school) text publishers.

I made inquiries, and miraculously landed appointments in New York. I visited with several publishers who were so generous with their time. After all, I wasn't applying for a job; I was simply trying to understand their business. Through our discussions, I learned about college textbook publishing, and how that part of the business was more suited for me. As a college textbook representative, I could work out of my home, and my territory would be the universities and schools in my area. For a single mom, this would give me optimal control over my schedule. I would work from a home office. I'd spend my days meeting with professors, learning about their teaching challenges and making every effort to demonstrate how our textbooks would address their problems. My goal was to "close the sale" by convincing the professor to order our textbooks for his or her class. That order to the bookstore was a "sale," and that would help me meet and exceed my business goals, generate company revenue and hopefully lead to a year-end bonus for me. I would have access to an incredible range of books to read. It was like getting another college education, free. It sounded sublime.

Not quite. The glitch: I would have to move from Maryland and start in a less-than-prime territory. I would have to earn the right to a prime territory. I would do that within two years, but for now, I was offered Pittsburgh.

This wasn't my choice, but I didn't have a lot of options. By then, I had been out of work for over eight months. I was thirty-two, and determined to get my life and finances back on track. My son's behavior had seriously declined, paralleling my own personal and financial decline. I had turned to his father for help but was rejected. I honestly thought that his father's home, now with two children (whom my son had never met), would be more stable for my son. But it wasn't going to be an alternative.

His father sent me to speak to a rabbi he knew of in his community. I took the Amtrak and rented a car to visit with the rabbi in New York. He told me he thought my son and I needed some space, but that clearly, his father's home wasn't suitable. He encouraged me to send my son to a boarding school in New York, and assured me his father would take care of the cost. That was how his father would help.

I have no defense for agreeing. It was imperative for me to get whole.

I would spend the next two years in Pittsburgh while my son attended boarding school in New York. Even though Rand McNally's magazine named it the best city in America to live in,

I never nested in Pittsburgh. In spite of the magazine's claim, I thought otherwise.

You might say I had one foot in and one foot out. My son and I visited often. I was already plotting our reconciliation and return to Maryland. I made only temporary, not lasting friends. I soloed.

The work came easy to me. I was successful. I opened a savings account. But a girl needs *entertainment*, and I met most of mine on the job.

HARDLY A BOSS MAN

It's curious how some things begin. When does a professional relationship become a personal one? When does a handshake become permission for a kiss? When does "Good night" become "I'll stop by your room at 10"?

As a field publishing representative, corporate folks frequently visited me. This included my regional manager and others such as the director of sales. Their visits were both instructive and evaluative. The Director of Sales, Boss Man, was complimentary. He was darling. A gentleman. We laughed easily and often together. We met at sales meetings twice a year. Our relationship could have been a spin-off from the movie and Broadway play entitled, *Same Time, Next Year*.

It did make the sales meetings more stimulating, but really rattled some people who suspected. Mixing business and pleasure in the workplace was prohibited by company policies. Even then, it seemed archaic for any company to have such outdated rules. After all, with increased numbers of women in the workplace and the reality that one spends more time at work than elsewhere, it's only natural for people to find each other at work.

Boss Man taught me so much about sales, and the knowledge and skills that would enrich my life. I enjoyed the intrigue, the sound of his incredible laugh and his tender touch. It was an authentic relationship devoid of emotional extremes and expectations. It ended gracefully with no regrets.

Smitten Calculus Professor

My regional manager was a different story. He was in desperate need of some serious sexual harassment education. But this was 1982, and the best defense for a woman was humor. I was good at it. Luckily for me, he never went beyond verbal annoyance. Unlike Malpractice Offender, I could endure his attention without threat.

While traveling campuses together, we stopped to speak to a math professor about our new calculus text. Calculus wasn't a topic I felt expert in, and I was stunned when this professor demonstrated such interest. My regional manager chided me as we left, telling me that we just closed the sale *only* because this professor liked me. Thinking, *He thinks with his anatomy,* I dismissed him. But he was right in this case.

The interest did seem to be a precursor for a dinner invitation, which I accepted. Smitten Calculus Professor was a Renaissance man, a brilliant academic with a love of culture and fine things. We talked a lot. As was and is my nature, I thought out loud, pondered the world, life, myself. He gave me a gift: the book, *Illusions: The Adventure of a Reluctant Messiah* by Richard Bach. His inscription read: *By showing me the messiah in you, I have hope of finding one in me.*

I found much-needed validation of my own worth and contribution as I read those words. I treasured the notion that I had "touched" people. But calculus didn't turn me on, and Smitten Calculus Professor didn't either.

QUIRKY ART PROFESSOR

Sometimes people just look like what they do. Bushy hair. Skinny. Frenetic. Jeans and t-shirt. Well-worn tennis shoes. Meet Quirky Art Professor. Platonic male pal.

Quirky Art Professor wanted to convince me how critical it was for me to understand art. I didn't want to learn. I preferred to be ignorant. I was a lousy student. My feeling was that when I see something I like, I like it. *What does it matter why?*

You understand. He didn't. He was disappointed in me.

I've always been more comfortable helping than being helped. Asking for help was painful. But I was alone in Pittsburgh, and asked Quirky Art Professor to pick me up at the hospital after I underwent outpatient eye surgery.

I didn't trust a man to accept me when I looked funny, failed, fumbled, was moody or flawed. Without the ability to trust, all I was capable of was *entertainment*. I couldn't put faith in a genuine relationship. Despite my best efforts at the time, fun and flight became my limits since I was unable to fully recognize and resolve my own issues.

I looked a little like ET, the famous alien of film, when I came out. It bothered me, but he didn't seem to care. For that day, he was the surrogate family and support system I didn't have.

Quirky Art Professor and I departed friends. He gave me a gift of a beautiful carved-wood apple, which adorns my home today. I proudly declare no knowledge of its artistic value. *When Harry Met Sally* was a film that portrayed the reality of "friendship" between a man and a woman. We were a regular *When Harry Met Sally* with a different and more believable ending.

HENNESSEY MAN

ISO ("In Search Of") was an acronym of the eighties. ISOs usually took the form of a personal ad.

On one of many warm summer days in Pittsburgh, I was bored and lonely. Not an uncommon feeling. I combed the paper for something to do and noted a singles ISO swim party. The prospect of meeting anyone at a pool party wasn't my ideal. Bathing suit. No makeup. Cellulite. Forget it!

But I decided to go—fully clothed, with no hidden bathing suit available to change into. I wasn't afraid of being refused admittance. I assumed (correctly) that the only prerequisite was to pay admission.

I met a man whose name escapes me. I do remember that he was an attorney and he liked Hennessey, an expensive liquor. Pleaser that I am, I always felt obligated to purchase whatever it was my date preferred, and have it available to offer when we went out. Not a bad habit, within limits. But, I was still a long way from understanding my own needs, and boundaries.

Not far along in our dating, it became clear that Hennessey Man wasn't worth the price tag of that investment. Without any parking tickets to resolve or other legal issues, he wore out his usefulness quickly.

MUSCLES

We met at a trendy wine bar that resided in an office building. I was alone, and had just come from a medical appointment. Even though covered with all the appropriate business attire, it was easy to see how physically fit Muscles was. Handsome, too. (I seemed to be getting better at this handsome stuff; it wasn't so threatening anymore.) Soon, I found out that he was younger than me as well.

Given the choice of brawn or brains, I would choose brains, I thought. That was my head talking, not my hormones. And this was beginning to have all the trappings of a "vacation romance," except that I was only in downtown Pittsburgh from the suburbs, not in an exotic, faraway place.

Regrettably, Muscles focused all his energy on developing his physique, not his mind. It was okay, as long as he didn't talk much. I was getting older and perhaps more impatient, if that's possible. I needed more.

Muscles seemed surprised when I wasn't interested in dating him any longer, and I had zero interest in enlightening him. This was one of those rare moments in my life when I didn't feel like being a teacher.

A FATHER: "CAN I BORROW YOUR DAUGHTER?"

Did you ever go out with someone when you liked his kids more than him? Toward the end of my time in Pittsburgh, I met such a man on one of my rare blind dates there.

The dental hygienist who cleaned my teeth fixed me up. The offer came while I was her captive audience, helpless to defend myself. One cannot talk when your mouth is being worked on, and even if I had wanted to say no, I wouldn't have wanted to offend her, given she had all the sharp tools in her hands. When she insisted I meet her friend, I gave her a strangled "Yes."

A Father and I met for lunch, and the restaurant just happened to be near a stereo store. I was in the market for a new stereo and into my pre-shopping stage (the current access to the Web has sharpened my process and cut down the physical time invested). A Father offered to come browse with me. He was helpful and appeared knowledgeable. A handy date: *always optimize the talents of the men you meet!*

We graduated to dinner next, and I learned a little more about him. A recovering alcoholic. Seeking new career. Divorced with a daughter. Stability was not his middle name.

Spending time with his daughter masked A Father's detractions. Given that my son and I were separated, I welcomed the chance to pseudo-parent. Never having had a daughter, this gave me a rare opportunity to do girl-stuff. I saw his daughter more than I did him. Though a quick fix and pleasant, it intensified my need to be with my son.

I had finally earned the right to leave Pittsburgh. To my surprise and gratification, I had transformed one of the lowest-performing sales regions to a territory that now claimed top-five status in our company. Even so, that achievement had cost me dearly. I'd been separated from my son, friends and the place I had come to know as home. I welcomed the opportunity to move on. I was eager to exit. It was easy to do.

Reversing Direction: Return to Maryland

*Life is a succession of lessons which must be lived
to be understood.*

Thomas Carlyle

I left Pittsburgh practically two years to the day after my arrival. I had landed a prize territory: Washington DC-Maryland. I was headed back *home*.

Life seemed to be moving in the right direction. I was pleased with myself. Back on my feet economically. I had received my first bonus check: a check for ten thousand dollars, which nearly equaled my annual salary. I made a copy of the check because it was more money than I had ever seen in my life, at least at one time. Always frugal, the money went immediately into my growing savings account. Three years later, I used it as a down payment for my first home, a beautiful three-bedroom townhouse.

But not all was good. The two years I spent living apart from my son seemed to damage our already fragile relationship. I had rebounded. He had not. I had perhaps denied or underestimated the short and long-term impact of him being in boarding school. He was angry and cold. I grappled with my feelings of guilt, accepted his verbal assaults and pained over his lack of affection. My much-anticipated happy reunion was never to happen.

Motherhood had been my childhood aspiration. I, like many other little girls, romanticized the vision. Married to achieve it. But I had failed to create the path to find that role as I had hoped. His acrimony remained the frequent dinosaur in the room. With age, the noise and acting-out lessened, but the punishment remained. My heart was and is still broken. I lost a best friend, hugs and dreams.

I had made it through Pittsburgh without one attached man in my life, and felt confident I was on my way to finding my soul mate. And to some degree, I was. But I overestimated my recovery. I thought I was through with *unavailable* men. Not so. There would be a few more regressions to bear.

My new home was in suburban Maryland, halfway between Baltimore and Washington, DC. A preferred location. I began a new chapter in my life. I remained in publishing, though not for very much longer. I was feeling rooted again, no longer like the embodiment of my favorite houseplant: a wandering Jew. This was my last stop.

Time would prove different.

Personally, I decided to examine my love-life strategy. First I revisited my *list*, much like Samantha had done in *Waiting to Exhale*. I committed to evaluating the men I met against my list without exception. I didn't want, nor could I afford to invest and waste any more of my precious time. I would stay focused.

At the time, it seemed logical to me to tap on the methods I had learned and used to foster my success in publishing. My first strategic act was to take a proactive approach to meeting men. This was a new city. A clean slate. Although I knew, then and now, that you never know when or where magic will occur, I wasn't going to just wait for accidents to happen. I wanted, and needed, to feel some control.

During my first official week as a resident, I attended a trade conference in DC. One of our booth's visitors was boasting to a colleague about his new bride, showing off fabulous wedding pictures. I couldn't help but notice, and tactfully commented and inquired. He had met his wife through a personal ad in an upscale Washington magazine. When he discovered my newly arrived and single status, he strongly encouraged me to do the same: if not place an ad, then at least answer one. It was an irrefutable argument; I could afford the price of a stamp.

His speech was effective. I was influenced, and decided to place a personal ad. Fancying myself as a writer, I thought, *This will be such fun! I can create myself.*

I labored over words, trying to get the essence of who I was into a few precious lines (your ad cost was based on the number of words). I had set a limit of spending no more than fifty dollars. In time, I got so good at this I actually wrote them for my friends.

Modesty is NOT a virtue when selling yourself. Meet me with two of my favorites, put into circulation on different occasions:

OPPOSITES DO NOT ATTRACT!

Only those passionate about living and laughing need reply!

New to (...)! I am a young-looking and young-at-heart (...)-year-old pretty woman who is both street/book smart, casual/elegant and strong/sensitive. My friends would describe me as spirited, fit, curious, communicative, reflective, romantic. I value humor, optimism and friendship. I enjoy healthy debate, music, dance and warm-weather sports. I am seeking a similar male to explore old and new. If you are a person who can savor the moment as well as plan for the future, please call or write.

NEWCOMER LOOKING FOR YOU IF YOU (like me):

. . . get younger and wiser each year; enjoy your own company as well as others; are interesting and interested; seek balance between work and play; value humor, romance, optimism, friendship, reflection; are strong, yet sensitive; are physically fit /nonsmoking with above-average appearance; more spiritual than religious. Please call or write.

When any one of my submitted ads finally appeared, I waited. They told me it would take at least two weeks till I got a "package" — packets of the letters that were sent to the publication (magazine or newspaper) in response to my ad. A fat package meant a lot of choices. A thin package would not be encouraging.

With time on my hands, I prepared a script for what I would say when I called the chosen few. My intent was to build on the ad, not repeat it. Keep them engaged.

Sample phone message for a person who responded to my ad:

Hi, my name is ... thanks for responding to my ad.

I'll assume you feel we are similar, so I'm going to share a little more about me, and if you are still interested, please leave a number and a best time to reach you.

First, everything I said about me is authentic; I live my words, so please be authentic too. I love the theater (musicals and drama best), dance, and music (jazz, popular, show are my favorites). I stay fit by exercising, mostly dance, aerobics, and warm-weather sports, not weights or machines. I am physically fit and want the same in my partner.

I think of myself as a lifelong learner, open to new ways of thinking and new things to know. Professionally, I am a (...). Optimistically, I hope to find a soul mate; realistically, I hope to find some new friends. Perhaps you. Now, it's your turn.

Covering all my bases, I also responded to some of the ads. I assessed what worked for me in the letters I received, and tried to capture those attributes: short, catchy and *clean*. That required a script, too, which usually began something like the following:

Hi, my name is ... and your ad caught my attention
There is only so much one can learn about someone in a few lines, but I will try to say enough that might invite you to respond, and then perhaps we can talk some more.

Then I would add some of my "walk on water" qualities (already mentioned in the previous letters) and close with:

If all this sounds interesting to you, please respond. I will be happy to share pictures at that time. You can contact me at...

When the "fat" packages of letters arrived, it felt like Christmas (more precisely, Hanukkah, a religious holiday of rededication that lasts eight days). Each letter was like a gift, a surprise. I reveled in such control of my fate. I could screen out the letters. I could further eliminate people after speaking with them. Out of the dozens of responses in each package, I did meet a few. In fact, over the years I met many men through In Search Ofs, print and Web-based. Here is a sampling of those I met through the print-only ads:

PENNY STOCKER
AND HIS BROTHER

Penny Stocker lived nearby. Normally, this would be a great advantage. Since I lived *outside* the Beltway, there were many times when I was eliminated from consideration for being "geographically undesirable."

When told by others that I lived, "far away," my reply would be, "Far away from what . . . you?" But I would think, *I live exactly where I want to be.*

Predictably, Penny Stocker rambled forever about penny stocks. His ranting seemed liked a foreign language. (This was before I became investment savvy.) However, I did already know that *healthy lifestyle* was important. Despite my ups and downs with weight and my struggle to stay slim, I could never get turned on to a guy with big gut. And this, he had.

Penny Stocker also had a brother who lived in Northern California. Shortly after we met, I was leaving for my annual publishing sales meeting that turned out to be in his brother's backyard, California. Good sport that he was, he "graciously" fixed me up with him. Timing is everything.

Penny Stocker's brother lived in my part of the world — the part I'd always felt connected with, spiritually speaking. Our meeting location was south of San Francisco, not far from Carmel. Reflections of the past. My California Dreamers. The place I was transported to with Rose Man, my first love following my divorce. So much history! So many memories!

Penny Stocker's brother had curly hair, my favorite. Contrary to his brother's, he had a tempting body. We drove down Big Sur. We *connected*. Romance. Adventure. Vacation privileges.

So much for my strategy of eliminating unavailable men. Regaining my senses, I knew that "unavailable" does include "geographically unavailable," and this he was. Farewell.

TOO FRUGAL A FELLOW!

A clear negative sign of any date is when a man doesn't buy you a bagel. As an experienced first-dater, I had rules about these first meetings with strangers. I never made assumptions. When I met someone, I would always offer my credit card to cover my drink or meal. If it was accepted, the handwriting was on the wall. So it was with this fellow, too.

Not only was Too Frugal a Fellow cheap, he was oddly bald. I envision that he didn't look much better with hair.

Cheapness drives me crazy. I have never been a woman of means. I have struggled financially most of my life. I would approach the mail with trepidation of arriving bills, and tremble with worry over unexpected expenses (auto, medical, etc.). I hid my inner turmoil each time my son needed and asked for another few dollars for school trips or extracurricular activities. Anyone who knows me would say that I was very frugal and proud of it. But, frugal is *not* being cheap, just being careful. I judged that if someone was doing *high-level math* to figure out a tip in a restaurant, or visiting every supermarket on Sunday to collect on all the specials, it was an undisputable red flag.

(For anyone reading this book that may be skeptical, I did have a date with a chap who diligently cut out and collected coupons every Sunday, and then traveled to every supermarket store on Sundays to get the best prices on toilet paper and other staples. That too is beyond frugal!)

My hypothesis is that cheap folks usually are cheap with their heart as well, and experience proved that true. The older I got, the more important it was for a man to be generous with his heart and mind. So Too Frugal a Fellow, and others like him, were on my "don't waste time on" list.

FAMILY MAN

I have always loved children. To this day, I often tell others that I prefer children to adults. Their energy and honesty is so welcome. This was the main reason why I never thought to exclude men who had kids from my consideration. My son was in high school by then. Most of my peers had toddlers and weren't at the same life stage as I was. To eliminate men with children would have greatly reduced my potential pool of dates. Given this, and my fondness for kids, it seemed only rational to be willing to meet men who had young children.

Oddly, the majority of the men I had met and dated thus far didn't have children. Family Man was an exception.

We met at a Chinese restaurant. Very congenial. He spent most of our time together talking about the antics of his three *very* young children. Spills! Toilet Training! Toddler versions of common words!

Despite my proclaimed love and affection for children, the conversation bored me silly. And the prospect of having little ones around full-time didn't appeal to me. It wasn't a conscious decision, but on some level, I had become accustomed to my well-earned freedom from caring for tiny tykes and being a slave to their schedules and interests. Or perhaps I knew intuitively how incompatible life stages can cause havoc in a relationship. I have learned this lesson real-time in my current marriage: the source of ALL our challenges.

Chinese food fills you up, and then you get hungry later on. Family Man would leave me hungry. Better to end before we began. At least he paid for the meal.

UNIFORM POWER

He was my first policeman. A former Los Angeles detective, and this was the time of the O.J. Simpson trial. What an incredible inside view! He also had stories to share related to his current role as a high-profile security guard. Scintillating palace tales!

A police uniform suggests a different power than a corporate suit. Without saying a word, strength and courage are assumed, and we feed on our childhood stories of damsels in distress. I wanted to fall in love with Uniform Power. He made it so appealing. Always trying to please me. He went along with my politics. Even tried to eat raw vegetables like I did. And was so patient, waiting for me to be ready to transcend from friend to lover. (Please help me understand why that makes me feel guilty, as if I'm not delivering on customer expectations.)

When "the evening" finally arrived, the look in his eyes was so telling. I envied what he was feeling, but despite my willingness, I wouldn't be able to meet him at the same place.

Time and best intentions were never going to create the attraction I yearned for. I've already conceded to optimizing my date's talents as appropriate, but I have never used anyone. Reluctantly, I sent Uniform Power on his way.

FORMER SMOKER

I am a dogmatic non-smoker. Always have been, and long before smoking became the public pariah it is today. I wasn't shy to voice my view if asked, or even sometimes when not asked. Growing up, I used to hide in the only bathroom we had in our apartment when my trendier older sister had parties in the house. I was seeking protection from the smoke. I stopped being friends with a group of elementary-school girlfriends during junior high school (now known as middle school in most places) because of their smoke-filled parties.

I have never dated anyone who smoked. The thought of kissing an ashtray repulsed me. I got accustomed to telling others that I was allergic to smoke so they would be more accepting of my absolute position. I came to believe this as fact. Fortunately, today local ordinances and cultural opinions now speak with and for me.

So when this blind date told me he was a *former* smoker, I was already turned off. The awe-inspiring water view of our restaurant couldn't even influence my bias.

After being direct with him, Former Smoker tried to convince me it was in his past, and to convince me how foolish I was to allow that to stand between us. (We were not even near an "us" — we had just met.)

He pegged me as a small-minded person. I don't care; his teeth looked like he stopped smoking the day before. Habits leave their legacy.

This was a one-and-only meeting. I know how to say *no*, which admittedly is easier to do when the question begs such a black-or-white response.

Saying *no* seemed to be challenging for many of my single friends. They would hem and haw about how to say *no* to a man's invitations, responding by saying they have to wash their hair, or have other plans. They would worry about hurting a man's feelings. I always felt that was unkind, and would encourage my friends to reverse the situation, put themselves in their shoes.

"How would you feel?" I'd ask them. "What would you want the person to say?"

There have been so many times when men were less than candid with me, telling me little white lies, giving me excuses and runarounds. All this left me feeling bad, and ultimately, foolish. I didn't want decent men to feel that way, so I decided early-on in my dating life not to impose that humiliation on any man. I propose that to tell a man that I'm not interested is a *gift*. It helps to protect their pride. With as much generosity and sincerity as I could muster, I would respond to these offers with a statement such as: "I appreciate your interest in me, but I'm not interested in seeing you again. I wish you good luck."

A brief hurt early-on is so much easier than prolonged excuses that lead to humiliation.

LEGAL RESCUER

Another attorney came along at the right time. My intrigue with lawyers was yet to be satiated. None yet have demonstrated the intellect or poise of my film and television icons. This individual and I had been dating a few weeks. No intimacy. He was getting close to asking. A weekend away was in the making. His plans were stalled.

My son graduated high school and left for college in 1987. I was a young thirty-eight. For the first time in my adult life, I wasn't feeling the need to be there in the morning and the afternoon when he left and returned from school. I was liberated. The past few years, I was feeling free.

Not really. Once a parent, you are never free.

To date, my son's major in college had been beer and fraternity life. I'd known he had been smoking marijuana for years. Although not thrilled or supportive, I preferred knowing than not. I hoped the open dialogue would keep him from exploring further.

He had always pushed the envelope. The operative question for me while he was growing up seemed to me to be: *How close can he come to falling off the edge without destruction?*

Perhaps that's why when the phone rang that day and he was calling me from *jail*, I wasn't surprised. He and a few of his friends thought it was totally cool to drink beer and smoke grass while driving. A park police person pulled them over and now he, his friends and his car were no longer feeling cool or like partying.

As before, I bore witness to how the universe works in strange and mysterious ways. Fortuitously, people would appear on the scene and have the right skill set. At that moment, intimacy with my friend was the furthest thing from my mind. Getting legal advice was. When the phone rang this time, Legal Rescuer was by my side. Good timing. He helped. My son's case was dismissed. And Legal Rescuer and I departed as friends.

It took me two years to stop shaking every time the phone rang. I hoped and prayed my son was wiser. I feared my ability to rebound was weakening.

FAX MASTER

Moving beyond the ISOs...

Sometimes I think I am a magnet for the poor. I met my first husband at my cousin's bar mitzvah (a religious ceremony that marks the passage to manhood for boys turning thirteen) hosted by my uncle, the relative that "made it" in the garment center. The celebration was an elegant affair. All the waiters were young, good-looking college boys decked out in tuxedos. Very appetizing. Most came from wealthy families, and were out to have some weekend fun and extra cash. My waiter (husband-to-be) was in fact the "poor" relative, who was working for the income and not necessarily to meet girls.

My uncanny ability to attract the needy persisted. I was a poster girl for the Statue of Liberty. Put me in a roomful of all kinds of men, and for sure I will attract the one that is poor and/or socially or emotionally impoverished.

This particular scene was a fundraising cocktail hour hosted by an organization to entice volunteerism and contributions. Undoubtedly I was there for volunteerism. A fashionable-looking guy approached me. I soon found out that he was an entrepreneur, espousing the use of faxes. This was the eighties, and faxes were NOT a household word. Faxes were a mystery, as in, "How does paper fed into one machine miraculously come out of another machine far, far away?"

Fax Master was intriguing. I spuriously concluded he must also be brilliant, and already was taking as fact his implicit messages of how rich he would become.

Fax machines weren't the only first this man would introduce me to. During the dead of winter, when the air was chilly and the wind was blowing, he convinced me to join him in a friend's hot tub. Two things made me tentative: wearing a bathing suit, and wearing a bathing suit when it was freezing outside. But my fear of appearing wimpy emboldened me. Once immersed, I enjoyed the warmth of the water and the view of a starlit sky. Getting out was another story. I think hot tubs are nice, but overrated.

Holidays can be depressing and lonely for single people. They're like one very long Sunday. After a few dates, I eagerly accepted Fax Master's invitation for a family holiday dinner. We drove a distance from town to be greeted by many warm relatives and friends. In the kitchen, he taught me the history of the fat that makes the gravy memorable. For the first time, I saw a fireplace between two rooms, filling each with warmth.

His invitation made me feel special. That is, until his sister-in-law told me about all the other women he brought to similar dinners. Once again, my assumptions missed the mark. He was more air than substance, in more ways than one.

Maybe Fax Master went on to become rich. My first husband did. If rich was that important to me, then maybe I should have been more patient. Maybe impatience is my habit and worst enemy. Maybe, more likely, rich was not that important.

Fax Master and I parted on good terms. In fact, so much so, he introduced me to my next blind date.

WOUNDED PUPPY

You may have made the same observation I have about men who've been shattered by their last love. Suddenly, they are in touch with themselves and life. They become incessant communicators, sharing and disclosing more than you want or need to know. They act like wounded puppies, seeking constant comfort, solace and validation. In contrast, my response to despair and rejection was to seek out a thirty-two-ounce jar of peanut butter and a large box of extremely salty Ritz Crackers. Solace was food to excess: expressing my self-hate and disappointment with me!

It was immediately evident that this blind date was a wounded puppy. The indicators were blazing, but I chose not to care. Grief had caused him to lose twenty-five pounds after his love left him for another man. It *is* plausible I wouldn't have been too attracted to him if he hadn't shed those pounds.

Wounded Puppy was a cordial date. Scrumptious dinners. (Food is definitely a theme of dating.) Chivalrous. Appeared magnanimous. Our timing was to my advantage. My birthday occurred during the first month I knew him. He bought me a spa package. In return, I wrote his speech for his daughter's bat mitzvah (a religious ceremony that marks the passage to womanhood for girls turning twelve years or older).

Before long, Wounded Puppy's bias for hard liquor and gambling became apparent. Call me crazy or a snob, but there's something about a lust for hard liquor and gambling that turns me off. I think I must still carry the stereotypes of the movies I saw growing up, or my mother's messages are deeply embedded in me.

Our final adventure together was in Atlantic City. I should say the *new* Atlantic City. My memory of Atlantic City was as a child, loving the Steel Pier, cotton candy and bicycles. No thanks to "The Donald," Atlantic City is a different place today.

You would be correct to challenge my decision to say *yes* when he invited me to join him for a weekend away, given I didn't like him too much, and dislike drinking and gambling. Here is the sad, pathetic answer: I tend to be rather organized, and frequently accused of being "not spontaneous enough." Wounded Puppy called me late on a Friday afternoon and tossed his invitation like a *dare* to me, positive that my preference for order would cause me to say *no*. I called his bluff and said *yes*.

Wounded Puppy gambled. I slept and watched TV. He did manage to insult me further by suggesting that he never knew anyone who brushed their teeth so much.

What does that say about his partners? I wondered.

Spontaneous, yes. Miserable, yes. It was a long drive back. I was too intellectual! Too control oriented! Too reflective! Too serious! I vacillated between anger and relief as this guy was dumping me, no longer sure who had had the worst weekend.

I did gain an important insight that helps me to this day. A *quirk* is only a *quirk* if you don't share it with another person. Had he been more organized, or brushed his teeth more, I would appear perfectly normal. A shared *quirk* is actually experienced as *cute*. I would just have to find someone who shared my need to arrange spices and CDs alphabetically, and who accepted the fact that items in the refrigerator and pantry really do have a designated place.

I was a step closer to knowing more about myself. Arriving home never felt so good.

PRESIDENT OF THE BOARD

From the moment I moved into my townhouse, it was my womb. On good days I would come home and smile. On not-so-good days I would come home and sigh in relief. My home was my personal sanctuary. It sat on the corner, a prime location. The entrance to the kitchen was off the parking lot, and that made schlepping luggage, grocery and shopping bags so much easier.

Even better: for the first time, my son's room was down the hall from me with a door which, when closed, would prevent me from seeing how differently we organized our lives. From the time he was little, he seemed to find it more convenient to dump trash in his drawer than in the wastepaper basket next to his chest of drawers. Even though he went off to college six months after we moved in, and thus became a part-time resident, his room's location helped us both.

I loved my house. Even so, there was a transitory time when my house scared me. Shortly after moving in, I began hearing this chirping sound at night. I was clueless. Bravely, I captured one specimen for the pest people and was informed that crickets had invaded me. There are no crickets in Brooklyn, just cock-roaches. Like them, the crickets were not invited guests, and we promptly got rid of them.

New to home ownership, I volunteered to be on the home-owner's association board, assuming this would educate me. I also wanted to understand where my association dues were go-ing and, perhaps, influence how the money was used.

The president of our board didn't live in our subdivision. He owned a few of the homes as an investment. Over the course of monthly meetings, I thought I got to know him. President of the Board acted like he had a crush on me, and he finally realized the nerve to ask me out.

Easily wooed by men who seem infatuated, he seemed harm-less enough to me. On the board, he was this polite and professional person who enjoyed speaking about his children and religious beliefs. I mistook this as the behavior of a man of integrity.

Our evening proved different. After a rather ordinary dinner, he took me home. Feeling comfortable with him, I invited President of the Board in for coffee and dessert. I never expected him to think I *was* the dessert. He transformed, became someone else. Very aggressive. I felt in peril as his physical overtures continued to ignore my wishes. It is as close I have ever come to experiencing the threat of date rape. Torn between shock, strength and determination, I pushed him off and out.

There was no crime to report. There was nothing I could do. Colloquial wisdom seems to suggest that women provoke these aggressions. I examined my actions, questioned whether I had encouraged his unwanted behavior. I had not. Women don't "own" the problem of unwanted male aggression.

The remainder of my term on the board was uncomfortable at best.

BACHELOR

My time in Maryland composed many stories. Some of these were more serious, and went on to become bittersweet memories.

I represented several curriculum areas for my publishing company. Family and Life Services was one. This department didn't exist when I was in college, and the courses covered the gamut of lifecycle stages and issues. The hot topics of the eighties were the rising divorce rate, the impact of divorce on children and families, the demise of the neighborhood and the dispersion of families across state lines.

I felt like a walking statistic. I embodied those books. I made them come alive: young married; young divorced; single struggling mother. I resented the generalizations in those texts that condemned the children of divorce, and remained determined to redress the statistics. My son would be whole. I would be whole. Having one parent didn't necessarily mean disaster.

I kept saying this daily incantation to myself, hoping and praying that it would be so, wavering between optimism and denial, vying to somehow sanction my naïve life-choices to date.

One lovely spring day I found myself roaming the halls of Family and Life Services. I approached a door, knocked, and a male voice welcomed me in. Boyish-looking. My favorite curly hair. Skillful at being quiet, but flirtatious. I learned through the powerful informal grapevine that this professor, who was my age, had a reputation for dating his students. Very much a cocky bachelor. His being known as a ladies man should have deterred me. Unfortunately, it only served to increase Bachelor's attractiveness.

I had no illusions about my future. I never bought him a toothbrush, but I *did* get to know Annapolis, a wonderful town.

Like some other relationships, Bachelor and I played "volleyball dating." We saw each other sometimes, and then not. We called each other to serve as escorts when we needed one but were absent a special person in our lives. Convenient, comfortable, uncommonly adventuresome. This went on for some time.

Years later, I found out he did get married. *We had only been entertainment for each other,* I thought. *Why should I feel defeated? Why should it matter to me?*

But, it did. Those terrible adjectives I tried so hard to keep from entering my head returned. *Rejection. Unworthy. Not lovable.* I had once more been unable to capture the ultimate attention of a desired male.

OUSTED JOURNALIST: A MAILROOM GIFT

ABC University was one of my publishing clients. While strolling through their Journalism Department mailroom, I struck up a conversation with a professor. Instant and lingering eye contact. He was a journalist from South Africa, an Afrikaner who came to the States after being ousted for his point of view during the end of apartheid. He was studying journalism.

This *older* student became a *younger* lover, and the only potential rival to my Limo Guy. Although not my first younger man, it was the first time that I was the more highly paid person in a relationship. I had a job. Ousted Journalist was a struggling doctoral student.

Our first date was at my house. It was during the days when I still liked to cook. These days, I enjoy having guests but prefer someone else to do the cooking.

There is a lot to be said for the men of South Africa. I can still close my eyes and relive the passion. No one ever told me that I had a "unique" anatomy. I'm not definite that was an advantage, but it sounded superb.

Ousted Journalist was disarming beyond his sexual savoir faire. Brilliant and controversial. Our debates were exhilarating. I accompanied him to small dinner parties hosted by his fellow Afrikaner journalists. The cerebral sparring was pervasive. These were indeed historical times for South Africa. The parties also demonstrated the boundaries of male chauvinism in South African culture. Men barbeque. Women do not. Around him, even chauvinism felt good.

We had a precious few months together before we each went our own way. Ousted Journalist had neglected to mention his girlfriend, who lived in South Africa but decided to come join him in the States. This time, I wasn't interested in being the *off-girl*.

Several years later I met him for lunch. As with Insurance Man before, some memories are best held onto for their original fantasies and dreams. When you meet someone you were strongly attracted to in the past and haven't seen for a long time, the changes can be disappointing. The memory of that person, which might have offered comfort or escape, can evaporate when the memory proves to be more flattering and seductive than the person now in front of you.

WELL-ROUNDED CHEMIST

Just about the time my Afrikaner departed. I met the second person I almost thought would be *the one*. (The first was Rose Man.)

As I've previously shared, a big part of my job as a textbook publishing representative was to get my foot in the door of a professor's office and create an opportunity to "pitch" our latest texts. This particular fall, we had a terrific new organic chemistry text. Organic chemistry is one those all-important introductory courses. All-important because *one book* would be adopted for *all* classes. To get the book adopted was to get a big sale.

Just as with calculus, my personal knowledge of and fondness for chemistry was limited. Although a good student in high school, I vividly remember keeping little "cheat cards" in my pencil case with chemistry symbols and formulas for insurance during exams. Chemistry made me nervous. But here I was, getting ready to be eloquent and convincing on a subject I knew little about.

I knocked on the door of the professor who was the decision-maker. The door opened. We both stopped and stared. Pleasing to the eye. Short, but built. I couldn't tell what he thought, but I found out soon.

I am a sucker for attention. He was so endearing. Gifts. Flowers. Lots of *gaga*. Well-Rounded Chemist not only loved music, he knew it. When a classical piece would come on, he could name it, at the same time exposing my ignorance. I'd smile in admiration, hoping to appear impressed. This made him feel really good. When we went to dinner he would include instruction on how organic chemistry and wine were intimately connected. Discussions on wine interested me more than classical music. Coincidentally, the author of the text that got me in the door was also a wine connoisseur by avocation. Well-Rounded Chemist was romantic.

But I was cautious now. I had my boundaries. He was uncomplaining, persevering. Maybe even too much so.

After months of courting, we made love. He approached lovemaking with the same focus and patience he had demonstrated during our courtship, leaving me fully satiated and wanting more.

Shortly after, we escaped for a romantic weekend in New York. I started to experience extreme pain upon urinating. Well-Rounded Chemist immediately diagnosed me with cystitis. (Later, my gynecologist would name it honeymoon cystitis, a condition that occurs in women who have intercourse after long periods of abstention.) He fed me water and cranberry juice. I was cured, and so grateful. It also didn't hurt to be perceived by him as a woman who had little recent sexual experience. It made me seem purer.

I liked this man. I respected his extreme intellect. I had just about given up on having another child. Amenorrhea caused by low body weight had robbed me of a normal cycle. When I found myself pregnant, I was in heaven. Thrilled! He was not.

I refused to accept his reaction. I begged for time. Meanwhile, I read books on prenatal care, learned everything about pregnancy I didn't know when I was pregnant with my son. I took vitamins. I planned a nursery. Thought about names. Sara was my favorite. Simple, Biblical, elegant. Intuitively, I knew it was a girl. I could see her in my dreams. I talked to Sara, the growing person inside me. I did all this convinced he would change his mind.

He did not. Quite the opposite, he told me that he only had about ten percent to give to anyone, and I had it all. (Somehow, I wasn't flattered.) The rest was for his laboratory and his potential Nobel Prize (which by the way, I haven't seen his name announced yet). Children were not an option for him, and the only supporters I had for keeping the baby were my son and my doctor.

This is when my story gets worse, not better. I cried. I pleaded. I lost. Two months later, I did what he and most everyone else said I should: had an abortion. I will never forget the terror and trembles as I fell unconscious, grasping my doctor's hand.

I hurt inside to even write the words. I will never forget that moment—not because of a political or religious stand, since I support the right for women to choose. I hurt because I feel I should have been stronger. I should have *not* succumbed to his power, or my fear. I should have had the baby I wanted, not had the abortion.

I had been strong all my life. Why change, or give in now? Sorrowfully and irreversibly, I did.

The abortion propelled me into depression for over one year. Inconsolable, I sought help from several professionals. One was a psychiatrist that I visited for a first and last time. His opening words were like spears when he said, "Didn't you know that if you had had the baby, he probably would have come around?"

This did not sound helpful. His response was contrary to my understanding and prior experiences. Therapy was supposed to provide a safe place for a troubled person to speak their story out loud without judgment; to enable one to get "outside" their own head and negative thoughts, get distance so one could see their issues more clearly without messy emotions mucking up the view . . . and path out.

Ultimately, I got my tubes tied. Never again. Sara's due date was August 23, 1988. I remember it silently every year.

LOYAL FRIEND

Due to my relationship with Well-Rounded Chemist and a successful chemistry text, I was milling around the Chemistry Department quite a bit. I met another great professor, but I was already spoken for by Well-Rounded Chemist.

I subscribe to the definition of male/female friendship described by the character Harry in *When Harry Met Sally*. During one of their first antagonistic encounters, Harry explains there is really no such thing as a male/female friendship. According to him, one of the two always wants the other romantically, but suppresses this passion, submitting to the notion that it's better to have some part of that person than having none at all. Eternal, unrequited love. Loyal Friend settled for being friends. He became my confidant. We didn't share "chemistry," but were definitely symbiotic. When I fell apart after the abortion, he comforted me. We went to dinner and played board games. Loyal Friend was tall and muscular, and I felt safe around him. His embrace kept me warm. Like other men in my life, I wish I had fallen in love with him, not his colleague.

Loyal Friend reminded me of another good-natured soul I met on the administration building's steps on my first day of college. Someone who helped me study, and I went to the movies with. I knew he liked me more than that, but I didn't reciprocate. Despite all his friendship, admiration, credentials and promise (premedical school), I never considered him a potential husband, a lifetime candidate. His physical looks didn't excite me. I felt no lust. My own vanity impaired my vision. When I met my first husband-to-be and told this friend, he warned me that I was marrying for the wrong reasons. He accurately predicted what would happen. I wish I could find him and tell him he was right.

We all meet at least one bona fide *good guy*, and sometimes we're smart enough to fall in love with them. I frequently wonder how my life would've been different if I'd possessed an ounce of the wisdom that I do today.

.

Entertaining Europe

Simplicity is making the journey of this life with just baggage enough.

Charles Dudley Warner

Publishing was good to me in innumerable ways. People. Travel. Resources. Books. Learning. Nonetheless, I longed to return to teaching. To fill this need, I became involved in creating new sales-training methods and tools for my company. If an opportunity to *professionally* grow in this way had been available with my current employer, I would've pursued it and remained in the industry. But the prospect wasn't there. It was time to look for another job.

I didn't want to return to the classroom, and decided to transfer my passion and skills from the classroom to the boardroom. I enrolled in graduate classes in organization development and training, a relatively new field at the time. All the while, I voraciously read every professional journal and combed the want ads for potential jobs. I was stunned when I landed a position with a rather large homebuilding and mortgage company. I was going to be the assistant director of training. I gave notice to my current employer and prepared for a well-deserved six-week hiatus before the new job started.

Having never been to Europe, I decided that forty years was long enough to wait for the consummate companion. I had already traveled alone in the States. Why should Europe be different? I planned a birthday present to me: a trip to England, France and Italy.

CAFÉ MAN

While I was in the planning stages for my trip, my sister came to visit me. You might say she has a veritable New York personality. Always had a flair for clothes, makeup and style. Whenever she visited, she usually would want to go to a club, and I... accommodated.

I'm not a bar person for several reasons. First, I've already confessed my position on smoking. Add on that I only drink wine—and not very much, especially if I'm driving. Early-on in my post-divorce life, I was enlightened that not only did I *feel* out of place, but also *looked* out of place at bars. Perched on a bar stool, a well-meaning person informed me I looked like apple pie, not a club girl.

But this time I was feeling upbeat because of the new job and imminent trip abroad; clubbing sounded like fun.

We went upscale to celebrate my fortieth birthday (which seemed to be lasting much longer than its deserved one day). We connected with two likely suspects, and had dinner with them later in the week. After my sister went home, my gent stayed on a while.

I had not been out with a *blond* since a connection with a lifeguard I had while on a family vacation in Florida. At that time, I was twelve. This man was blond, tall, firm and *proud of it*. Café Man was the first man I knew who bragged that he didn't wear underwear. I never got that close to check out his story.

My recollection of Café Man is hazy, but while writing this book I was compelled to recover a European travel book he bought me for my first trip abroad. The inscription reads:

. . . . *have a wonderful, wonderful trip on the continent. Bring back lots of memories. You're special. "I travel not to go anywhere, but to go. I travel for travel's sake. The great affair is to move." Robert Louis Stevenson.*

I am certain that I read this inscription when Café Man gave me the book, but it didn't affect me at the time. Reading it now, I feel badly that I don't remember him as a poet. I don't remember how nice he must have been to me. He took me to the airport, and that adieu was the last time I saw him.

LITTLE BROTHER

My trip to Europe rivals my fantasy trip to California. Both had experiences beyond my limited imagination in store for me. (I could easily say the same for this entire book, since it describes a part of my life that, as a child, would have been inconceivable. My only future picture I had as a girl reflected a white picket fence, a station wagon and five children.)

My trip would embark in London, then move on to Switzerland, Paris, Venice, Florence and Rome. Like California, Italy was another dream-location. From childhood, I believed I was more Italian than Jewish. I *loved* to talk with my hands. I *loved* family. I *loved* wine. I *loved* passion. My first lover and teacher, Limo Guy, had been Italian!

I booked myself on an independent American Express trip, thinking that was just about the right amount of supervision for a first-time, single-female, European traveler. I deplaned at London's Heathrow Airport, and boarded a bus to the hotel. One undeniably precious-looking American male was on that bus and I shamelessly flirted, anticipating there would no such similar species waiting for me on my tour.

Much to my surprise, pleasure and fate, it turned out he was on the same trip as me, and on his way to meet his parents at the hotel. Recently divorced. Younger. And eager for a big sister. *Hello, here I am!*

We became this incredible, impermanent family. They made my travels of Europe unsurpassed, taking me places I otherwise would have never seen. Little Brother's mother was born in Lido, and we visited her home. His father was a retired military man, and we visited Anzio, a sleepy fishing town that bordered a well-known American cemetery for World War II veterans. Every meal was a departure from the normal tourist traps. Little Brother and I went on the gondolas. We went to theater. We walked on the Seine. He introduced me to Baileys Irish Cream, and it became our ritual every evening after Mom and Pop went to their room.

And somewhere along the way, I wanted to be thought of as more than a big sister. I wanted him to desire me, but I could tell he didn't. I kept my rejection inside, not wanting to spoil our time. I feared that disclosure would scare him away.

After twelve glorious days, we boarded separate planes, and having served each other's needs well (for the most part), made no plans to meet again. It was a most unforgettable holiday.

From Europe to Turmoil

Be bold. If you're going to make an error, make a doozey,
and don't be afraid to hit the ball.

Billie Jean King

I returned from my European vacation eager to begin my new career in homebuilding and mortgage. I arrived at my new office, asked for my boss and was shocked to discover that he had been abruptly terminated—and with that news, any hope and expectation I had about my work life and future vanished. The person who hired me had apparently fallen out of favor, and I knew it was only a matter of time before the ax would fall on *me*.

I correctly predicted my fate. Within three months, I was on the street looking for work.

I was at a crossroads. Returning to publishing would be the easier route, but I decided to weather the storm and stay on my current professional track. I wouldn't return to publishing, but remain focused on creating the future I pictured.

Luck would prove to be on my side. First, I leveraged my Masters of Reading Education and took a job teaching, piloting a preschool language arts initiative. This bought me time and paid the bills.

Then I tapped into my sales success in publishing to secure a position as an account executive (salesperson) for a corporate training company based in Texas. I would be responsible for their Maryland/DC region. This was a strategic decision. I banked on the hunch that my prospects and clients would be the very same people I was hoping would hire me. That a great job would soon be on the horizon.

To my amazement and delight, I found myself at one of the largest hotel chain companies within a few months. I had landed *the dream job*. I began as director of program development, then assumed the role as one of several internal training and development consultants. I was assigned a specific region, comprised of twenty-two hotels.

Early-on, I attended a major conference for all of our hotel general managers. More than two hundred twenty hotels were represented. One general manager leaned over toward me and, in jest, told me that my "future husband" was in that room.

He misspoke. Who was in that room became the utopian *love of my life,* but never my husband.

UTOPIAN LOVER

If you've ever read the book *Soul Mates* by Thomas Moore, you know that it's almost impossible to put into words what I felt about this man. Completely taken. Volumes of words spoken but unsaid.

The first time I saw Utopian Lover smile, I did not, could not understand what was going on. Neither did he. True understanding would have been impossible, perhaps even undesirable. It would have gotten in the way.

Utopian Lover was my client. We met often, spending hours discussing and debating the critical strategic initiative I was supporting his hotel with. One evening, sitting opposite each other in a restaurant booth, he blurted out, "I love you."

My heart came to life and stopped at the same time. Before me I saw an Adonis, a near-perfect man. Beautiful in every way. And he loved me!

He was married. We should have stopped then. Utopian Lover wanted to, or at least he said he did. I didn't want to. Any rational thinking was abandoned at the prospect of having this love in my life. The inevitable jeopardy wasn't considered. I thought he was my soul mate. I had no choice but to follow my heart. I believed all the challenges and contradictions would be resolved. I ignored their power. Utopian Lover succumbed.

This one decision spiraled our lives out of control. Instinctively, I knew he would stay married. Time would prove that Utopian Lover wasn't courageous. That he couldn't fathom how he could be with me and not lose his children's love. His vision of any future with me was limited by what he saw as two unacceptable choices, one negating the other.

For many years we were *on* and *off*. As the years passed, more often than not, I became the one who wanted, needed out. Each time I left he would cry, promise a future, and his words would get me back. He cornered me at airports as I was boarding, called me long-distance if I was traveling, and stalked my home.

I wanted so much to trust him. I wanted so much to be with him. I was positive that all my suffering would be worth it if we could find our way to be together. Hope became expectation.

There had been other unavailable men in my life before, but this was different. Utopian Lover met my friends and my family. We finessed how to be clandestine. We were heroic in our efforts. We traveled. We celebrated holidays.

The first gift he gave me was a keyboard. Early-on in our conversations while probing to know all about each other, I shared my missed childhood wish of playing a piano. He heard me, and the keyboard was his way of trying to fill that empty space. I felt known and accepted.

We shared extraordinary moments, times that words cannot do justice. And yet I can hardly remember one moment that wasn't clouded or compromised by the ever-present agony of our cloaked, fluctuating status.

Others were quick to tell me that our love, our relationship was a sham, a delusion. We were having an *affair*. For it to be authentic love, one would have to be openly coupled, married, living together, battling daily hurdles and still able to see stars and shiver inside with anticipation.

Now married and looking back, I know they were right. Yet romantic love disguises another's blemishes. Its lure prods us recklessly forward. At the time, no other person I had been with, made love to, made me cry with joy when we were complete. Utopian Lover's mere presence touched me that deeply. Its trance caused me to neglect my boundaries, my hopes, and my *self*.

I knew then and now that to feel that way isn't healthy. I endured great pain, loss and anguish each time Utopian Lover and I separated. In the end, the only way that seemed possible to finally sever our emotional ties was to leave. To leave the state, not just the relationship. This emotional roller coaster had taken its toll. My only choice was to leave the place I'd come to call home, where I felt rooted after so many years of feeling adrift. Where I felt comfort.

Pain is a great motivator, and so I did.

Ironically, after I sold my townhouse and relocated, Utopian Lover was transferred to another city. Had I been more patient, I wouldn't have needed to uproot. But patience has never been my virtue.

The distance didn't accomplish all I hoped. After I moved out he visited me several times. He sent me birthday presents. He called and e-mailed. It would take more time and another man for me to finally be able to say *no* and mean it. But I stopped responding to him. Caller ID and e-mail made that easy to do. When I finally did reply and told him I was remarried, he was silent. The messages stopped.

While writing this book, I heard from Utopian Lover again. He claimed he was calling because he wanted my advice on a business venture. During our talk he quietly, but with an earth-shattering sound, told me he was separated.

I thought about that a long time. *Separated. Not divorced. People who are getting divorced don't use the word "separated." Separation is an experiment, not a commitment.*

I surmised that Utopian Lover was baiting me, trying to see if I would grab the hook, drop my life and be his again. That wasn't going to happen. I was wiser and happier now.

For a moment I chastised myself for even musing the thought. Then I quickly delighted in the POWER of not asking; the POWER of not caring anymore; the POWER of discipline and the pride and satisfaction of knowing I had found a better place for myself.

During the ups and downs, ins and outs, ons and offs of this tumultuous relationship, I was fortunate to have a few good male friends that deserve honorable mention. I confess intimacy with both men, but it was always more out of our friendship and comfort than the guise of romantic love....

COLLEGIAL COMPANION

I first met this man during my time as an account executive for the Texas-based corporate training company. I was manning our trade booth at a conference in Florida. The first morning, a pro-fessorial-looking type visited us. He stopped to chat and left with his free goodie bag.

(Getting free stuff tantalizes many people. Everyone mean-ders the corridors of trade shows for the goodies. My own husband cannot resist free food in supermarkets, or similar items. Thanks to his business travels, we will never run out of hotel shampoo and soap.)

I thought I had seen the last of our guest, but he came back at lunch. Then mid-afternoon. And conveniently showed up at the end of day. Unbeknownst to him, Collegial Companion tapped on my weakness for men with curly hair, and off to dinner we went that night. And the next. Turned out he lived in DC, my geographical neighbor.

When we returned home he invited me to join him for lunch. Sounded good to me. We met at his office, and a subtle wave of his hand dropped the news: a picture of his wife and daughter. My assumption that married men wore wedding rings was clearly fallacious. Another lesson learned.

I went to lunch explicit about the boundaries of our relation-ship. He was a consultant, and we did similar work. We had lots of professional things to talk about. Our collegial friendship grew.

One of the many differences I've pondered between men and women is a man's uncanny ability to compartmentalize every-thing. Forgive my indulgence in generality, but men can be very much married, even claim to be in love with their wives, and still want to make love to someone else. This may account for why

Collegial Companion felt it perfectly okay to desire a sexual relationship too.

On a few occasions, this became a reality. Usually when I was so down, rejected by Utopian Lover and feeling angry, resentful, frustrated and unfulfilled. Vulnerability and need of comfort is a lousy-but-truthful excuse.

Collegial Companion's creative and clever way of getting past our obvious barriers was to introduce me to phone sex. It sounds trashy, but after I overcame my tremendous reticence, I found it quite erotic. There I was lying in bed alone, and *he* was on the other end of the phone. Quietly, seductively, he narrated—with emotion—what he felt about making love to me. The description created a pleasing picture in my head, and I grew to like this. Perhaps I *was* fooling myself. That this wasn't *really* having sex.

Unknown to him, Collegial Companion was my only phone sex partner, a recognition that might have been meaningful for him.

Perhaps a more important recognition would be the lesson Collegial Companion taught me about the meaning of commitment: albeit his interpretation differs from mine. A decade later, I would come to accept how one must mentally as well as emotionally *decide* to stay with one person. That this is a prerequisite for relationships that last.

Collegial Companion was reliable and consistent. His empathy and willingness to listen and accept me, despite my stupidity, was solid. He never lectured me. I loved that in him.

LIVING INSPIRATION

Another job change. It was now the early nineties. Reorganization and Total Quality Management ruled. My role with the hotel chain company was eliminated, and I headed for the consulting world. My first affiliation was with a small boutique firm. It was there that I encountered one of the most inspiring people of my life.

It began with an impromptu job interview in Pennsylvania. I was facilitating a session at a national conference, and my colleague there recommended I meet with this man. As an experienced interviewee, I became aware that our conversation was lingering, and delving into nontraditional topics. That we were both engaged with each other. This led to a new job and finding an unequivocal best friend.

A VP of a successful firm, Living Inspiration was also a former Navy pilot as well as a cancer survivor, since he'd fought and survived lung cancer ten years before our meeting. In his presence, one would never guess that he had to take several prescriptions daily to keep him alive and minimize his pain. To see him was to see a tall, fit, and amicable person. He was a triathlon competitor. To speak with him was to hear only words of friendship, caring and support. Not needing to demonstrate power through impact and volume, his voice almost a whisper. Never arrogant. Never a grumble. Living Inspiration wouldn't be defeated or deterred. His enviable strength was understated but not unnoticed. He lived in Wisconsin, and distance and frigid climate separated us. But when we were together for business or spoke by phone, I felt worthy.

By now you can tell that there were many men in my life. Many were pure *entertainment*. Once in awhile, someone enters who stands out and makes you feel validated. Living Inspiration was the one for me.

GOOD SOLDIER

Big Management Consulting Firms were actively recruiting people like me. Although skeptical, one made me an offer I couldn't refuse. From the start, it was apparent that I didn't fit in. Round peg in a square hole. Everyone, including me, was keenly aware of the misfit. To declare my individuality, I added a third pierced-earring hole in my left earlobe to differentiate my appearance. (Two holes were fairly commonplace in the nineties.)

A colleague and Good Soldier of the firm approached me with his apprehension for my future. Although no longer feeling like a waif, I must have retained a bit of my innocent appearance, looking like a fair maiden in distress. Good Soldier wanted to protect me against my uncontrollable, relentless will to tell the partners how little I really thought about them. He also warned me to stop saying that the firm "raped" their clients of money and staffed people to make profit for them, not the client. He wanted to teach me how to survive, even prevail. I wasn't interested. I didn't want a window office.

I trust his intentions were honorable. I also think Good Soldier had a fancy for me. I have already admitted that weight is an issue for me. I prefer my men a little taller and comparatively heavier than me, just enough so I can feel like the thinner person. Too heavy isn't good. Too thin always makes me feel fat. (Talk about being picky.) Good Soldier was a big man, too heavyset. He lived in Chicago and suffered an additional strike against him because of that, since there was no future for a warm-weather person like me in his beloved Windy City. My relationship with both the man and the company would come to an end, yet both had served me well. Change was on my horizon again, but before I leave Maryland, let me share two of my memorable *single* vacations….

Club Med...
A Single Woman's View

No one can make you mad, sad or glad but yourself.

Anonymous

W here do all the singles go? Club Med. Club Med.
My first Club Med vacation had been with my first husband, and was the place where I met my Maryland best friends. But Club Med's rightful call to fame was that it was the place to go when you were single. Within a month after our separation, Husband Number One went there. He left sad and came back tanned, cavalier and energized for his new life. No more tears for him. The power of Club Med!

To me, it was like adult camp. Attractive, scantily dressed people worked the Club as the GOs (gracious/gentle organizers). The guests were the GMs (gracious/gentle members). It was affordable. The clubs attracted people from all over the world; it wasn't likely that you'd meet a single mate who lived nearby, geographically. (Long-distance relationships are costly, rarely survive and hardly worth the investment.)

At Club Med you could drink without worrying about driving. You could also try any sport just for the heck of it. I remember standing in line for a thirty-second chance to learn how to water-ski. I had no interest in water-skiing, and to this day wince at the prospect of putting my head under water. However, I stood in line countless times just for the sheer pleasure of being held by one gorgeous GO. (To learn to water-ski, the instructor has to wrap their arms around your waist.)

Oh yes, the power of Club Med.

SIMPLE GUY

I have not been known to be impulsive about anything that costs money. Men, yes. Money, no. So when I decided to go to a Club Med over one Fourth of July, it was completely spontaneous: one of those rare departures from my *normal* self.

My son was at camp. I felt alone. With one call, I was booked and on my way. This would be the first of several vacations to Club Med I took during the *off*-times of my two decades in Maryland.

I wasn't nervous about the trip. I was skittish about an un-known roommate—one of the downsides of traveling alone. The Club will assign you a roommate, and that had no appeal. I liked my privacy, and didn't want the pressure of having to compro-mise my living space with a stranger. Lucky for me, I got acquainted with a great gal at the Houston Airport: our main check-in and transfer point. We became fast friends, and by the time we arrived in Mexico we had agreed to be roommates.

Vacation romances are in a class by themselves, short-lived but welcome diversions. My *list* went by the wayside; my stan-dards were dramatically reduced. No worries about tomorrow. That was this trip.

Simple Guy was a sweet, proper, younger guy from my fa-vorite coast, California. No hanky-panky for us. There was beach-walking, sitting on the rocks, moonlight boat rides and enjoying the envy of those other single women who didn't luck out. A non-threatening yet fabulous trip.

My single sister was also a vacation partner. One of our trips was to another Club Med in Mexico. It turned out to be double fun, double platonic....

FITNESS MAN

This trip to Club Med coincided with one of the coldest weeks in the year in the States. My sister was coming from New York, and her plane was extremely delayed. I arrived at the Club first.

Even our Club in Mexico was feeling the effect of the freeze up north. Outdoor activities went inside. Many were replaced with substitutes. That first day, I went to an exercise class and chanced upon Fitness Man. His mat was next to mine. We glanced and flirted each other's way. He seemed older but well preserved. Athletic. Full of himself. And all of this was visible without a word being spoken. Rule-less vacations permit attributes normally avoided in your real life to become charming.

We hardly had a serious conversation. Just fun! A duet in karaoke and dancing; competitors in playing Tequila Jeopardy (a takeoff of the popular television game show, where the reward for correct responses was a shot of tequila).

But this was all temporary. Fitness Man was geographically remote. He lived in Canada. A friend to share the week, but no more.

SENSUAL SABRE

There is something about a Sabre (Israeli native). They exude a potent strength, virility, and demeanor. We came face-to-face at the pool: my least favorite place to survey romantic prospects. This time, I was clad in appropriate bathing suit attire. (It didn't matter how much I dieted or worked out; once a chubbette, always a chubbette.)

But Sensual Sabre was searching for comfort, not a perfect ten. He was in the throes of a "tentative" separation from his wife. (I think he was tentative, and she more certain.) At any rate, he was seeking friendship. At Club Med, that's an easy thing to do. Group meals are open to all. You have to work on being alone, since practically everything is outdoors. There are hardly any places to hide.

Sensual Sabre had his two stunning sons with him, and the group meals we shared felt like family gatherings. This is what he wanted most. That, and a willing ear. Our talks felt like therapy sessions. Me the counselor, he the patient. Sensual Sabre was living in New Jersey at the time, but destined to return to Israel, as well as to his wife.

Although a single feels less conspicuous at a Club, it still holds all the minefields of any singles event. There is hope, and disappointment. *Will I meet someone to have fun with? Will I be alone?*

I have been to Club Med married and single. I'd rather be married.

Winds of Change: Heading South

When one door closes another opens: but we often look so long and so regretfully upon the closed door that we do not see the one which opened for us.

Alexander Graham Bell

I had much to be grateful for my experiences with Good Soldier, as well as the Big Firm. Those experiences created both the opportunity and financial support for me to relocate and become an independent management consultant. When I went out on my own and entered the world of the self-employed, my dismay over their business practices made it easy to identify a tagline for my business. *Consulting with Integrity* was how I wanted to be known by *my* clients. Now, my only challenge was to find the best place, and path, to accomplish that goal.

Destiny steered me to Atlanta. It wasn't even on my short list of possibilities. Phoenix and San Diego were my first choices, but fate had other plans. My association with the small boutique firm had ended after two years. The company was imploding. My inspirational friend left for new ventures. As did I. My son had moved to Atlanta five years earlier, immediately upon graduating college. Growing up together had been a difficult haul. We had been close, but in a distant way. I was the first person he called when he was in trouble. I was the first person he called when something great happened. If he had led a typical life, I probably wouldn't have heard from him much. When he left home, we were both ready for the space.

Leaving Maryland was my strategy to end the revolving door with Utopian Lover. The unanswered question was where I would go to invest my energy for *this* new life. I was visiting with my son while deliberating my future choices. Over dinner discussion, he shared that he also was at a crossroads professionally. Perhaps he felt empathy. Unlikely as it sounds, I'm almost certain he suggested Atlanta as an option. And I'm equally certain that he sometimes regrets his charitable offer.

But as luck would have it, a firm offered me both a job and

relocation to Atlanta. The answer to my query became self-evident. The pieces of the puzzle merged naturally together. *Atlanta it is.* I left Maryland, a home that I loved and lived in the most years since my divorce.

When the last carton was loaded on the truck, I stayed on and sat in my now-empty house. I thought I'd be filled with loss, grief and sadness. I surprised myself, because what I felt was hope and strength.

I left with another new resolve. No more unavailable men. No more meaningless relationships. I must know: *Can I have a relationship? Do I really want to get married? Am I capable? Can I live and love in the mundane, and abandon my persistent lust for adventure?*

I was consumed with self-doubt. I knew I could attract men, but *could I go beyond that?* My failures and disappointments happened because of my lack of discipline, courage and boundaries. I accepted complete responsibility. But I hungered for something better, and I was determined for it to be different in Atlanta.

With clarity and intention I returned to the personal ad strategy I employed when I moved back to Maryland. I planned to network, attend functions, and get the word out that "a new woman is coming to town." This was the fourth time in my life I was relocating. Each time, including this one, I barely knew anyone in my new hometown. My key contact in Atlanta was my son.

This time, I was so focused that I actually went out with men from Atlanta before I moved there.

LADIES MAN

Throughout the years, one of the ways I tried to stay connected with my son was to hang with his friends. I was younger in age, lifestyle and spirit than many of his friend's parents, and found it easier to fit in, if in a slightly different role. Perhaps a bit more honest: I knew they were drinking beer, not lemonade. I knew they were sexually active. I tried to encourage responsible choices. I felt close and accepted by his friends, sometimes more by them than by my own son. They were kind to me, and I appreciated their interest and affection.

After my decision to move to Atlanta, one of my son's friends took my picture to his boss. A single guy. He called, and before my actual move we went out during one of my interim visits. Ladies Man introduced me to fantastic restaurants that remain favorites. He was one of those men I felt on the fence with. I was attracted, but not overwhelmed. Historically I wouldn't have bothered, but now I wanted to get to know him better and challenge my personal questions and self-doubt. But Ladies Man's door never opened that way, so that wouldn't happen.

I suspect that this nice, ordinary man was experiencing a Don Juan-midlife crisis. Scoring was important, and I don't just mean getting laid. His goals appeared to be playing the field, mounting up numbers of dates, and enjoying the juggling of multiple partners. His twice-weekly aerobics classes proved a healthy and handy resource for his ongoing quest for new women.

Playing the field definitely didn't fit *my* new criteria. After a few amusing evenings, before and after I moved to Atlanta, we elected for friendship. I became his backup date. When Ladies Man had a ticket for something and needed a date, my phone would ring. Like my relationship with Bachelor, it was a deal I could live with.

Occasionally, I bump into him at social functions. Still unmarried. Most of his belles have moved on. I wonder whether he regrets his self-indulgence and fear of recommitment.

PHOTOGRAPHER

Before I was officially a resident, I updated my personal ad and placed one. Atlanta doesn't have an upscale magazine, so my only option was the newspaper. Though skeptical, I decided to hazard it.

Most of the responses weren't audible. Some sounded like they spoke another language: foreign, or perhaps just very Southern. Or, perhaps my Northern elitism was surfacing.

But amongst the slew, there came this sexy voice. I promptly called, and we met during my next visit. My five-three height made me feel like a midget to his over-six-five stature. As we shared wine and food, he spoke of his world as a photographer and his interest in seeing me again. Atlanta was starting off well.

We resumed contact when I arrived permanently a few weeks later. Photographer helped me settle in, and lent his skillful insight on how to arrange my pictures. My newfound strategy had surfaced a striking, engaging beau. We experimented in my new kitchen, window-shopped and explored restaurants. Photographer became my first Atlanta lover.

Time would tell that this tall man was more wrapped up with his young daughter than interested in me, and that my optimism would prove premature. I invited him to my company Christmas party. He said yes, only to cancel right before the event due to a sudden conflict with his daughter.

Holding firm to my personal commitments, off he went. But I still needed a date....

PONYTAIL DOCTOR

After I moved to Atlanta, I assumed my son could be my backup date. If I had theater tickets and no one to go with—he was it. Sounded reasonable to me. Sounded awful to him. He would go to any lengths to avoid it.

Now dateless for my company party, I let my son know that he should get the tux I'd purchased for him cleaned: at my expense of course. He was desperate not to go with me. So desperate, he offered to find me another date. My only criteria was that the mystery man could dance.

And dance, he did. A jazz club was our venue for our break-the-ice meeting date before our party rendezvous. His ponytail struck me, but I wasn't sure how. It wasn't clear to me whether this was a positive, neutral or negative impression. I'd never gone out with someone with a ponytail. I refrained from jumping to conclusions.

Between music sets, I learned that Ponytail Doctor was a sole practitioner psychiatrist who had abandoned the benefits and challenges of modern health plans (PPOs and HMOs) because of hassle and cost. Ponytail Doctor's car was a distinctive fifteen-year-old in need of replacement and a thorough detailing, in part contributed by his cherished large dog. The dog was older than the car.

I'm not certain if Ponytail Doctor was suspecting my curiosity or testing my comfort zone, but at some point during our evening he literally let his hair down. I don't mean he divulged his inner secrets, but untied his ponytail. A part of me was envious of the texture and wave of his long, flowing hair. Another and equal part of me was uncomfortable . . . and now viewed his ponytail as more appealing. He seemed like a leftover from the sixties. Definitely a free spirit.

I was beginning to get weird vibes, but desperation prevented me from backing out of our party plan.

Like a caterpillar transformed to a butterfly, Ponytail Doctor appeared looking like a magazine model when he picked me up for our black-tie event. A complete metamorphosis. I could feel all eyes on us as we entered the ballroom. The hosting company was extremely conservative, and the feisty rebel in me reveled in the shocked looks on people's faces. We danced every dance. He was incredible. Our bodies joined fluidly in rhythm as he led me through every dance. We hardly spoke. The night ended. It proved to be an ideal arrangement.

Welcome to Internet Dating

*The way I see it, if you want the rainbow,
you gotta put up with the rain.*

Anonymous

W ithout a reputable local magazine to place personal ads, I turned to the Internet. I was computer savvy and computer-dependent for work, but to date had never considered using the Internet as a resource to place or respond to ads. I'd been strictly a print person. Now I decided the Internet was just another way to meet new people.

I was about to embark on new territory.

I identified a few sites and scanned them. As a visitor, I could browse but not buy. Searching and contacting required membership. Even so, browsing helped me eliminate sites that didn't offer geographically desirable prospects, or single men of my age group or faith. Finally, I selected a few sites to enroll in.

This proved to be a demanding process. The first step was to complete a lengthy questionnaire. Then came the critical decision of how long to sign up for: a range of one month to one year. Optimistic, I usually opted for three months.

Once enrolled, I prowled more seriously. It was like going shopping — tall men, blond men, bearded guys, sports enthusiasts and more. When I saw a picture I liked, I clicked open their profile and read for more information: clues to their real self.

I answered many, many ads. Instead of receiving packets of letters I sometimes heard, "You've got mail!" Pictures were often attached (several taken ten or more years earlier). The progression went from e-mail to phone talk, and then maybe an e-date. I adapted all my previous scripts to meet this new technology to help me determine if I should consider the gamble of an actual meeting. Here are some revised questions:

? *How did you come to use the Internet?* (trying to get their background)

? *What has been your experience so far?* (What they liked and didn't like could be an indicator of their success.)
? *What has been most disappointing? Surprising? Satisfying?*
? *Have you found that people look like their pictures?* (a good lead-in to setting up an expectation for honesty)

My investment yielded multiple but limited opportunities. Here is a smorgasbord....

MODEM MAN

I had no picture to guide me as I entered the restaurant trying to look cool and calm, and at the same time scan the room for my e-prospect. Satisfied that there were no men alone anywhere to be seen, I visited the ladies room for a last-minute face checkup, then returned to the waiting area. Hardly a moment passed when one of two men I'd seen together at the bar approached me and introduced himself as my e-date. I assumed his buddy at the bar meant that he made friends easily. We found seats and began chatting.

We all know how that first date goes. "So, what do you do?" (Or in layman's language, "How do you earn a living, and how much?")

He told me he was in the computer business, but now was looking at other lines of business. His most recent venture was a rock music bar — which let me know we didn't share music tastes. He described his homes, former homes and former wives. The picture he created for me on those subjects seemed more opulent than affluent. I also found out that the man he was speaking to was his personal driver. Suffering from a rare eye disorder that was causing him to slowly go blind, he was unable to drive any longer. I was impressed with his candor.

Sometime around dessert, a light bulb went off in my head. It occurred to me that his last name is embedded on the inside of most computers... a veritable Modem Man. His celebrity and infamous story was quite engaging, even if he wasn't. However, e-dating has presented its potential.

TOO POOR A MAN, POOR MAN!

My alter ego has always been on Broadway. Growing up, I would blissfully seclude myself in my room, lock the door that had no lock, and belt out the lyrics of George Gershwin and Rodgers and Hammerstein. My single happiest high-school memory was participating in our annual theater production where, like Barry Manilow, "I wrote the words and sang the songs."

Given this, I've always been receptive to anyone who offered free show tickets. I agreed to this e-date without much qualifying.

The theater was very bad; the seats were in a mediocre arena. Poor Man was an average type with a less-than-average job, car, home and personality. Money had never been on my list as a high-priority value; however, at the risk of sounding either shallower or wiser, it gained my respect with age. I didn't necessarily want a man who earned more (though that would have been nice), but I didn't want someone who earned less. Although I had been my sole breadwinner for most of my adult life, I didn't want that role, responsibility or control in a romantic relationship.

This person was not for me. I was pleasant, but not so nice that I encouraged him to call again. Having by then reached almost-expert status in dating, I'd mastered the art of letting men know when I was interested or not. However, many of us, men and women alike, lack the ego strength to recognize a rejection when it presents itself. That's why I wasn't so surprised when Poor Man called and asked to see me again.

But there would be no acting, or pretending. I wouldn't mislead Poor Man or give him any reason to linger, have hope or invest any more emotional energy in me. As I had learned upon my return to Maryland, saying no was my *gift* to him.

PONYTAIL TIMES TWO

Coffee bars are ideal settings to meet e-dates. Coffee is a short commitment, though tough on your breath if you should get lucky.

I met my second doctor who donned a ponytail at such a local place. Both were psychiatrists. A possible theme emerged, and I speculate that I'm one of few women who can claim to have two blind dates that were both psychiatrists and wore ponytails.

Recognition was slow to come by, since Ponytail X2 didn't live up to his picture. He had more hair, less brawn, and his taste in clothes had faded since the photograph.

Ponytail X2 was a decent soul who provided more details than I cared to know about his chosen professional life at a state mental hospital. He went on to whine about divorce, children and money. *Likes their job* was an original list item, and men like this one were immediately eliminated from further consideration. Given his profession, I wondered how people who are *openly uncentered* profess to be able to help others.

Hello. Black coffee. Goodbye.

CRASH SURVIVOR

Sometimes I would read an ad, and the words seemed to jump out from the web page and grab me. Secretly, I'd hope this unknown person would be a similar spirit. That was the ad I was looking at now.

I made contact and worked through the protocol to the next step: making a phone call. I tentatively dialed the number, a part of me excited, a part of me fearful that the voice would disappoint.

After listening to a smooth voice speaking near-perfect words, I left my message and waited. *Will he call?*

He did, and after a brief conversation, we agreed to meet for lunch. I'm feeling giddy.

As usual I arrived first, and eagerly scanned every diner who entered. An attractive man walked in, and our eyes connected in mutual acknowledgement. He presented me with a dozen red roses, and I was taken aback. Lovely, but premature. *Perhaps I'm just being skeptical*, I thought.

We sat opposite each other in a restaurant booth. Before our lunch was ordered, he whipped out this picture album and flipped it open. With animation, he walked me through his life-changing event. Pictures tell the story. A stormy evening. His car goes out of control, turns over and over. It looks like a heap of metal. And he walked out with barely a scratch to become a whole new man.

Born again to something, but I wasn't sure what. His monologue seemed to go on and on, through ordering, eating and paying the check. Not once did he ask me a question about me. Crash Survivor appeared a self-proclaimed celebrity.

My excitement fizzled. Somewhat letdown, I took my roses home and continued my search.

HANDICAPS & OTHER OMISSIONS

By their definitions, blind dating or e-dating brings uncertainty. One need not disclose every wart and pimple on the telephone before you meet, but there's a hope and assumption that people will be relatively honest, forthcoming.

For the most part, the men I met were truthful. The most common offense was a picture that captured a younger version. But there was another omission that bugged me. We all know that everyone is lovable and deserves to be loved. But I do consider it less-than-truthful when a blind date fails to mention a noticeable physical malady. Two e-dates that were remiss in that way rivaled the uniqueness of encountering two pony-tailed psychiatrists.

Man One showed up wearing a very corrective shoe set on a large lift. I tried to act as if I didn't notice. During dinner, I boldly broached the sensitive question and asked what was wrong with his foot. He educated me on a malady that I was previously clueless about. It wasn't his condition that turned me off — it was his deception coupled with his extremely thin physique. (I have already confessed my discomfort with skinny men: They make me feel plump.) Both provided me adequate rationalization for rejection.

I arrived at the restaurant before Man Two did, and was soon experiencing that queasy, sick feeling in my stomach I always get when waiting for a blind date to appear. I positioned myself coyly at the door so I could monitor approaching diners — a game of "hide and sneak a peak before they see you." I hovered at the restaurant entrance, searching the parking lot for potential men who might be my date.

And then I see him. I know at once. This man walking toward me has Parkinson's disease. I can see him shake from a distance.

We met, and sat for dinner. After the predictable amenities, my curiosity prevailed over my awkwardness. I came straight out and asked, "How come you didn't mention your Parkinson's disease to me before we met?" Then I leaned back and awaited his answer.

He replied that his therapist told him that his affliction wouldn't matter with the right woman. She advised him not to inform his dates.

I told him that his therapist underestimated the impact of omission as an element of trust. My heart felt bad, but I wasn't the right woman.

BIGOT

Bigotry is heinous to me. Always has been. I was a sixties college girl, and participated firsthand in the turbulent times of civil rights and political assassinations. My view was and remains that prejudice is equal to ignorance. If only we all could be more educated!

The television movie *Roots* premiered the summer of 1976, the same year I first moved to Maryland. Annapolis was shown as an original port of entry for the slave ships. I was shocked and appalled to find out that I had moved to a *slave state*.

Atlanta is in the Deep South, and sadly, many people I met still harbored some nasty and negative attitudes and beliefs. Too many remnants of hate and racism thrived. I did my best to avoid these people and places.

Rarely did an e-date turn up wearing a sport coat. This one did. He shared his strong condemnation of business casual, holding it in part accountable for the demise of the workplace. He believed that employees had become increasingly less productive and presentable, and this directly correlated with company policy that endorsed wearing casual attire on the job. I, among others, didn't share his point of view. He boasted that he dressed properly with a jacket and tie each day, despite his peers. I'm sure he stood out, alone, and enjoyed his lack of camaraderie.

Bigot lamented the old days in more ways than work clothes. He crowed with pride how he would travel to a shopping mall ten miles out of his way in order to avoid the mall closer to him that had become "too mixed." I was torn between slapping his face and attempting to civilize his pathetic soul. I did neither. His outlook was an unfortunate reminder that the worst of the Old South was alive and well.

Now I tend to visit the mall he avoids, an assurance I won't bump into his sorry face again.

CYBER LOVE

Occasionally, stories of true e-love are journalized on morning and evening television magazine shows. My track record to date didn't suggest that this was remotely possible. *How could you fall in love with a picture and a voice?* I'd think. *Is true love possible to find on the Internet?*

Finally I decided that online vendors served these advertised success stories up as a luring fantasy to urge membership renewal.

I don't know what compelled me to respond to a personal ad for a person who lived in Michigan, a wintry state. It was foolhardy. But I did. It was his biography; he was a dean of a college, an academic. I felt a kindred spirit.

Cyber Love and I communicated by e-mail and then shared pictures. I was so nervous when I sent my picture. I couldn't bear to hear his verdict. His approval was a welcome relief. I was surprised how turned on I was when we spoke by phone. Casual conversation felt sensual. I'd never met this man, and as it turned out I never would. Cyber Love's home and work were nonnegotiable. As were mine.

We avoided the inevitable and made plans to visit. I bought new sheets, a sign of my unspoken intentions and hopes.

Fortunately (I think), before we greeted each other at the airport we woke up, came to our senses, faced our reality and knew this wasn't a good idea. No future. No purpose. Cyber Love remains a mystery, but one that makes me grin and wonder.

I didn't put all my eggs in one basket: I decided to venture beyond the Internet....

The Old-Fashioned Way

I can change only myself, but sometimes that is enough.

Ruth Humlecker

SOUTHERN GENTLEMAN

I discovered a group called the Singles Golf Association. It seemed irrelevant that not only didn't I *play* golf, but I also didn't have any interest in *learning* golf. What interested me was that they held monthly parties and conducted golf clinics. I decided to attend.

My thinking was that this would be a worthwhile endeavor for two reasons. It seemed likely there would be a higher percentage of mature folks attending (my age group), and that these attendees would *also* bring a prerequisite income capable of playing golf. (I knew from friends that this was no cheap sport.)

Right on both counts.

The first and only man I met was born and bred in the Deep South, in a location some sixty miles north of Atlanta. His hometown was so small that the street he lived on bore his family name. Our initial pursuit grew predominantly from curiosity, not passion.

Southern Gentleman walked and talked with all the naiveté of a visitor to the Big City. I was his first Jewish friend. That was engaging for him, not me. Southern Gentleman's dialect was hard to understand, and couldn't be attributed to the fact that I've been deaf in one ear since I was eight years old. He called me "ma'am." Amusing, but uncomfortable.

I began to approach this relationship as if I was conducting a research thesis in Anthropology 101. I visited his home. I met his eighteen-year-old son and feigned communication. (I could understand the father; his son was unintelligible.)

I heard tales of Southern Gentleman's childhood. He spoke freely and defended his Southern heritage. Slavery, for him, was his childhood nanny, who he loved, and she was part of his home. She was happy, and he claimed not to understand what all the "noise" was about.

My Yankee roots kept protesting as he postured that other people "just misunderstood." North met South.

If this wasn't sufficient to move on, Southern Gentleman also was impotent. Impotency was a growing trend in the men I met, a sure reflection of my age group.

I didn't meet "Mr. Right" through the Golf Singles. I did gain two other important things. One was the absolute knowledge that I cannot play golf. Although superb at hitting balls that soared high and far at the golf range, I was useless on a course when the ball had to go in a *specific* direction to a *specific* hole. The other acquisition was a dear girlfriend who shared my embarrassment at not making many a par.

SAILOR MAN

I had created my own birthday tradition when I gallantly traveled to Europe on my fortieth. To avoid the loneliness that usually accompanied my passage of age, I would go on a vacation. Most of them centered on something I like to do. Like going to a spa for a week. Or in this case, tennis camp in my favorite state: beautiful California.

I arrived and scoped out my week. I searched for safe activities I could explore as a single woman. Fond of jazz, I ventured out my first Sunday afternoon to a local jazz club. *How dangerous could an afternoon be?* I reasoned.

It proved not to be dangerous at all.

I arrived early and secluded myself at a corner table, positioned to see the door, the bar and the music. I expected to relax with wine and music, and feel proud of my courage to chance out on my own. I had zero romantic expectations.

In he walked.

Sailor Man was both sexy and shy; I could tell this immediately. Intense combination. Distracted, I found myself searching for his eyes, seeking a connection, an opportunity to flirt. Suddenly he was approaching me, and I flinched; now I would get exactly what I'd been silently wishing for.

Abandoning my criteria for relationships *and* my strategic focus, I agreed to have dinner that night, and every other night of my trip. Sailor Man was a local policeman (quite different from the life of Uniform Power, my LA cop), and living an easygoing life with one overriding passion. That was sailing.

My birthday was definitely not about feeling lonely.

Sailor Man and I stayed in touch after I returned to Atlanta, and on my next trip out west (I conveniently had a client in Canada at the time!) we met in San Diego for a terrific weekend. I overcame my fear of drowning, and actually begin to enjoy sailing. Another weekend in Vancouver by way of San Diego, and the truth triumphed. Sailor Man gave me an exotic wrap-up from a recent sailing trip... and also made it clear how uninterested he was in an exclusive relationship.

So, where is this going? I thought. *How will this help me achieve what I want?*

I couldn't afford to fall into the snarl of a long-distance *and* unavailable lover. That was my promise to myself.

Au revoir, adios, arrivederci to my Sailor Man.

New Capitalist

I had an occasion to lunch with a friend of my son's and his parents. We had a fine time together — so much so, they wanted me to meet a single male friend of theirs who lived in town. This friend had been a buddy of theirs for many years. They had all participated in one of the popular groups in the seventies that helped people get in touch with themselves. Some considered these groups cultist. They preached a lot; had their own kind of language; seemed to espouse superior ways of being and thinking.

Most people, like this couple, kept their participation as an avocation. This friend had been earning his living for years as a teacher and speaker for the group. They told me that their friend had finally abandoned his role in pursuit of more money. Capitalism prevails! Now he was working for a consulting firm and packing the bucks in. I had no objection to the fix-up.

Several nights later, the phone rang and a deep voice introduced himself as the friend. New Capitalist was calling from the bowels of Canada. Cold as heck. Far from anywhere.

We went through the typical niceties. Then, unlike some others I've mentioned in this book, he tells me straight out that he suffers with sleep apnea. I am illiterate, so he fills me in. It seems that this condition causes him to sleep with a mask on to breathe, and he informs me that any woman who loves him will live with that mechanical barrier to spontaneous kissing.

What could I do but agree? Fearful of behaving in a shallow or ungrateful way, I accepted New Capitalist's invitation to dinner when he returned to Atlanta.

Another profoundly tall man. And big. He also had an instruction and insight for my every habit. If I was picky about my food, he cautioned me on the issues that must be contributing to my obsession. If I expressed my view about men, women, sex and commitment, I was admonished on how antiquated my thinking was. If I was curious why a single man who just recently left modest means suddenly needed a five-bedroom house and a wall devoted to a TV screen even though he was never home, I was reprimanded on my attitude. I even got informed that my front door didn't fit my personality. New Capitalist escorted me to a nearby Home Depot so he could show me what would be more suitable.

I love school and learning, but I wasn't feeling educated: I was feeling attacked and patronized.

Sleep apnea wouldn't have kept me from a man I loved. I know this to be true because my current husband sleeps with such a mask for the same reason. What drove me away was New Capitalist's inability to accept anyone with any ideas outside of his own. New Capitalist may have left the cult, but he never stopped the evangelism.

BOARD MEN

When I was forty-eight, I discovered I had osteoporosis. A life-time of dieting had robbed me of a regular menstrual cycle. Now I had fragile bones: a silent and deadly disease. I could write a book on this topic alone.

In addition to exercise and medication, I dealt with my prognosis by becoming an active advocate. I joined a nonprofit board to raise money and awareness to fight this insidious, prevalent and preventable affliction that affects one out of every two women over fifty.

Board members are an eclectic group. There were two men friends at the first board meeting. They sat next to each other. Mutt and Jeff. Those weren't their names, but their apt metaphors. Tall and short. Chubby and scrawny. Average and cute-looking. I found out later that they sort of flipped a coin for me and Short, Scrawny & Cute won. The only other time in my life that two boys fought over me was in junior high school. What an incredible piece of flattery at fifty years old!

Short, Scrawny & Cute was a printer, and had volunteered to provide in-kind support for our posters, and collateral. We dated a bit. He was divorced and living on a shoestring. His business was going downhill. He economized by not turning the lights on in his house. He had two small children. Life was hard. I was beginning to feel more like a therapist and mother than a woman on a date. Not an uncommon role for me.

The one thing Short, Scrawny & Cute was proud of was his sexual prowess, which he attributed to his previous profession as medical anatomy artist. Envisioning lovemaking with him felt mechanical, not passionate. He also admitted fascination with sex shops. I realized that I had lost the bet. Maybe the other guy was a better choice. I decided to find out when Tall, Chubby & Average asked me out.

Tall, Chubby & Average was reminiscent of the guys that

have it all right on paper. Easygoing. Generous. Comfortable. Children out of the house and on their own. I tried to fall in love. And I tried some more. But I could no longer pretend. NO passion or charisma.

I know he had a different story. When I told him we were done, he complained how he had *changed his life* for me.

I still don't know what he was talking about. He didn't move. Didn't give me money. His retort remains elusive. I can only conclude that Tall, Chubby & Average must have an incredible imagination.

Shortly after, the board dissolved, and so did our friendship.

This coincided with my son's marriage. I was without a serious lover to share this incredible wedding weekend. In truth, I didn't need one. All I needed was to see the joy on my son's face and the hope in his heart. For the years I had lived in Atlanta, I had tried so hard to meet someone, to meet the right someone, obsessively seeking to validate (or not) my own self-doubts about my capability to have a sustained, lasting relationship. I had tried in vain. And now I was finally ready to stop trying.

The Pickle Man: An Unexpected Arrival

The greatest happiness of life is the conviction that we are loved, loved for ourselves, or rather loved in spite of ourselves.

Victor Hugo

THE ONE

I love the movie *Crossing Delancey*. In fact, it's the first videotape I ever purchased. It is a *girl* flick. The main character, Isabel, is a young woman who has escaped her roots on the Lower East Side of Manhattan for the sophistication of the Upper West Side. Actually, she's more than left her roots. She harbors a haughty disdain for them, convinced she's risen above them.

Isabel's bubbe (grandmother) is concerned about her granddaughter's pending spinsterhood, so she arranges a meeting for Isabel the good old-fashioned way. Isabel is appalled—her proposed match is a "pickle man" from the old neighborhood. What was her bubbe thinking? A pickle man, someone with smelly hands and clothes. This was an unglamorous job, and everything an uptown girl would *not* want.

Out of love for her bubbe, Isabel agrees to meet this stranger, but is quick to set him straight to avoid any misunderstandings.

The pickle man is as frustrated as he is persistent. Desperate to show his love, desperate to get Isabel to *hear* him, he's at a loss on how to speak with her. For him, it's as if they live in two different worlds.

Bubbe is cleverer than her erratic speech and behavior would have one believe. And not at all modest. When she was young and oh-so-pretty, she flaunts, all the young suitors wanted Bubbe. Courted by many, she chose one, her now-deceased husband.

What distinguished this one from the others? It seems that this man sat on a chair before her and wouldn't budge. Still. Like a rock. Immovable. Unshaken. Relentless—until Bubbe said yes.

Bubbe knew that *this* man, a man who wouldn't budge, would always be there with her and for her, through thick and thin, sweet and sour, easy and hard. With her infinite wisdom she tells Isabel's suitor: Persevere, and you will prevail.

He does, and finally finds the way to Isabel's heart and mind.

Isabel finally hears him and more important, hears *herself*, perhaps for the first time. Like her bubbe's, Isabel's pickle man was the man who wouldn't budge, the one who would always welcome and love her for who she was, not for who she was trying to be.

I watched this movie with smiles and tears, wanting to find *my* pickle man, someone who would be that steady, consistent and loving. But like Isabel, I couldn't hear him, because I couldn't hear myself.

In January of 2000, following my son's fall wedding, I attended an all-woman conference sponsored by a friend and colleague of mine. I had never been much of a women's conference-type of person. But this wasn't just a conference about how to be assertive. Rather, it was targeted to professional women as a venue to meet, congregate, network and attend business sessions that would enhance their already notable achievements. My friend and colleague was persuasive; I felt cornered, and agreed to not only attend, but give a presentation.

Let me digress for a moment. This very friend had been dating a man for about eleven months prior to the conference. Whenever we got together, she would chat about him. I had the impression they were good friends more than lovers. He had accompanied her to the previous year's conference, and suggested that a special session might be offered to speak to the needs of the few men (spouses and significant others) that showed up with their female partners. On the spot, she recruited him to design and implement his suggestion for the next conference.

She also told me that, about the time she pushed to gain my agreement to participate, she ended the romantic part of their relationship. Romantically, she was on to new and greener pastures. Yet although the relationship was over, their friendship was not, and he was keeping his commitment to run the for-male-only workshop.

All of this meant nothing to me at the time.

Being the only male, he was easy to pick out in the registration room; I spotted him upon arrival. From across the room I thought his shirt looked torn, and decided it would be a gracious gesture to let him know and avoid him undue embarrassment. The only one embarrassed was me: It turned out that he was wearing a customized shirt designed for maximum ventilation, the type of shirt only a fly fisherman would know about. Fishing is a sport I was and remain ignorant of. To this day, he boasts I was flirting. I vehemently deny it. It's a playful debate neither of us intends to win.

We met again that first evening, but more formally this time. Since we were there because of the same mutual friend, we both gravitated to her dinner table. He was looking and sounding a lot more adorable, and I was starting to get those inexplicable, uncomfortable knots of attraction in my stomach. Of course, I successfully resisted acting on them. By now, these feelings scared me more than engaged me.

Our fates began to collide. The next morning, I found myself behind him in the breakfast buffet line. It was a slow wait; he was grabbing most everything in sight.

Afterward, we sat together, and he consumed all the foods I don't eat— bacon, sausage, eggs, etc.—while I munched on fruit and yogurt and tried very hard not to comment on his food choices. Months later, he would profess that he fell in love with me over breakfast. And my reply was that I almost fell out of like at that moment. *Healthy lifestyle* was a high priority on my *list*, and his choices appeared anything but healthy.

I was scheduled to conduct a session on gender communication. Since this works best with men, I took advantage of the opportunity and invited him and his small company of men to participate. They did.

Introductions are a standard way to begin any workshop. Two people with the same, unusual last name were conspicuous. It became evident that his former wife, who was also at the conference, was also in my session. At first, I thought that was more comical than instructive: divorced spouses together in my gender communication session. I didn't pay much attention. I should have.

The session came and went, and we planned to meet again for drinks before the evening luau. All-inclusive resorts are both blessings and curses. Free food and drink. He had been taking full advantage. My drinking capacity paled compared to his demonstrated ability to hold his liquor. I was definitely the cheaper date.

There was an undeniable attraction. He was ingratiating, amusing and pleasing in an innocent, subtle way. Noticeably attentive. I was enjoying this. I begin to loosen up. This wouldn't be my first vacation romance. Long-term commitment or compatibility didn't ever enter my mind, but vacation fun did.

That's what I thought it would be. Mistaken again!

He left the conference a day early with a promise to call me when I got home. He did, and we started dating. Our first date was memorable. He lost my telephone number and was running late. In a frantic sweat, he called our mutual friend to salvage what he hoped would be an auspicious beginning.

Over dinner, we discovered how much we had in common. Not about sports, which I gathered was his sole passion. But about values. Not about our interest in food or alcohol, but about family, fidelity and commitment. Not about music—his bias was for rock, mine for jazz—but about friendship. Not about our different work styles—he being the good corporate soldier, mine the rebellion of routine—but about laughter. And the list went on.

We were getting serious fast. Too fast. There were many legitimate differences we needed to explore. We were at different life stages. I had a grown-and-married son. He had a preteen and teenager. We shared different religions, and I didn't want an interfaith house.

Our getting to know each other was abruptly halted. Despite the care and actions I took in response to my diagnosis of osteoporosis, I suffered a spontaneous hip fracture in April, 2000. It

was the first evening of Passover, a religious holiday and celebration my new beau was looking forward to as his first Seder
(the name of the meal on this occasion). Instead, we were in the
emergency room. It was surreal. This could not be my body. This
could not be *me*. The fire department and emergency technicians
transported me to the hospital. My only menu choice that night
was major surgery.

This one incident changed our relationship. After five days in
the hospital, I came home. I was in constant pain. The left side of
my body was swollen three times its normal size. Staples, the
likes of which you see on UPS boxes, lined my left thigh and hip.
Hives covered my body in an allergic reaction to morphine. I
wasn't a pretty picture. He applied salve to my wretched body.
He kissed my sores. Unlike any time before in my life, I was no
longer experiencing my pain alone.

I walked with crutches. First two, then one. It took three
months to walk on my own again. None of this seemed to faze
him. I cried frequently, more out of fear than discomfort. He lis-
tened and held me. He never complained. Observers might
incorrectly speculate we were a married couple of twenty years
than a couple of barely three months. His love and patience were
unconditional.

He was and is my pickle man. He redefined love for me. He
wouldn't be deterred. He wouldn't budge. When he proposed, I
accepted. I wasn't naïve, but hopeful that our mutual commitments and strength would equip us to deal with all the
uncertainties ahead. We were married one year and one month
after we met.

And challenge did and does come. Repeat surgery. Econom-
ics. Family. All of the usual daily trials and tribulations and then
some. And through them, the open and honest communication
coupled with devotion to our vows has served to strengthen and
nurture our love, not diminish it.

Marriage is the ultimate seduction. We are drawn to the
promise of possibilities, not a record of proven accomplishments.

Being happy is a desired but elusive and vacillating emotion. I have come to define a good partnership not by the more common measures of happiness, but by how much one feels more confident, stronger and secure. Successful marriage diffuses our worry of weakness, and trusts that our partner will not only tolerate, but embrace our imperfections. Mutual vulnerability requires courage, and is the priceless blessing of love and marriage.

It is a gift to wake with a man who finds you beautiful in the morning, who kisses your face as you sleep and tells you, in actions that words could never match, how much he loves you.

The words I spoke for our toast at our wedding capture my *One*:

Your love is a gift. Because you love me, I have discovered caring, trust and intimacy in ways I never experienced before. I have come to know you:

- 💜 *The romantic who showers me with affection, loving cards, beautiful flowers, tears of joy and laughter.*
- 💜 *The man who shows me your commitment to our relationship by really listening, communicating and working through the tough stuff.*
- 💜 *The man who can wipe my tears, and hold me silently when I hurt.*
- 💜 *The father who loves, cares for and yearns for his children, a father who embodies parenthood.*

I have come to know and love all of you: my husband, my best friend and my lover, and hope that we will always have the wisdom to love and enjoy each other in the lifetime we have together.

It only takes *one*. If you have found him, treasure him. If you have not, don't give up.

Final Reflections

This is the last of human freedoms, the ability to choose one's attitude in any given set of circumstances, to choose one's own way.

Viktor Frankl

T he men in my life have been the theme of this book, but as it evolved, the book was more about me than my men. Each man contributed to the tapestry of my life: each man a thread of a different color that created my cloth.

I traveled the real-time journey of a girl with a simple childhood vision that evolved into a complex, different life. I have lived mostly unmarried. I bore one child, not five. I searched for answers to questions I never knew could exist. Strength, courage and conviction became my life mantras.

Lyric and song have paralleled my existence. I have no need to reinvent great words. I find comfort in the lyrics of "I Did It My Way."

Unlike the lyrics, I did (not) "carefully chart each step." Would I do things differently? Probably.

Like the lyrics, "Regrets, I have a few, but too few to mention," I made the best decisions I could at the time I was making them.

I have no complaints. I have no embarrassment. I have no shame. To quote a great woman, Eleanor Roosevelt, "No one can make you feel inferior without your consent."

I wish this for you, too.

I feel pride. Pride in my resiliency. Pride in my willingness to assume personal responsibility. Pride in my intentions, although my outcomes didn't always match them. Pride in my authenticity. I spoke the "words I really feel and not the words of those who kneel."

You, too.

The men in my life were good to me and good for me.

You, too.

The adventures memorable.

You, too.

The life lessons I learned were invaluable. From Entertainment *to* Insight.

You, too.

I hope you have enjoyed these tales and saw parts of yourself and your story in them. Writing them put a smile on my face, hope in my heart and filled me with gratitude.

Perhaps you, too.

Thank you for listening.

About the Author

Rochelle Turoff Mucha was married at nineteen, a mother at twenty, divorced at twenty-four and remarried at fifty-one. For twenty-seven years, she lived the *real* world of a very typical single woman struggling to find her way. Professionally and personally she connected with women of all ages, and their stories spoke volumes of shared loves and losses. Rochelle hopes her book will be a source of *entertainment* and *insight* for others.

Rochelle was born in Brooklyn, New York and currently lives in Atlanta, Georgia with her husband, near to her grown son, his wife, precious granddaughter and her second husband's lovable children. A published author of dozens of professional articles, Rochelle is founder and owner of Consulting with Integrity, a management consulting firm that focuses on organizational strategy, leadership and learning. Her expertise includes interpersonal communication, mastering change and individual coaching.

Printed in the United States
17052LVS00007B/91-366